I Am A Nuba

09 11299164

Renato Kizito Sesana

I Am A Nuba

Paulines
Paulines Publications Africa

I AM A NUBA
© St Paul Communications/Daughters of St Paul
ISBN 9966-08-179-8
Year of publication 2006

Original Title: IO SONO UN NUBA © 2004 Sperling & Kupfer Editori S.p.A., Milano
Translated by: Silvano Borruso
Cover photo: Giovanni Todeschini

PAULINES PUBLICATIONS AFRICA
Daughters of St Paul
P.O. Box 49026
00100 Nairobi GPO (Kenya)
E-mail: publications@paulinesafrica.org
Website: www.paulinesafrica.org

Cover Design by Elizabeth W. Rioba

Printed by Kolbe Press, P.O. Box 468, 00217 Limuru (Kenya)

Paulines Publications Africa is an activity of the Daughters of St Paul, an international religious congregation, using the press, radio, TV and films to spread the gospel message and to promote the dignity of all people. The books published, however, reflect the opinions of their authors and do not necessarily represent the official position of the congregation.

Contents

South Sudan Louks office)

Sudan – Political

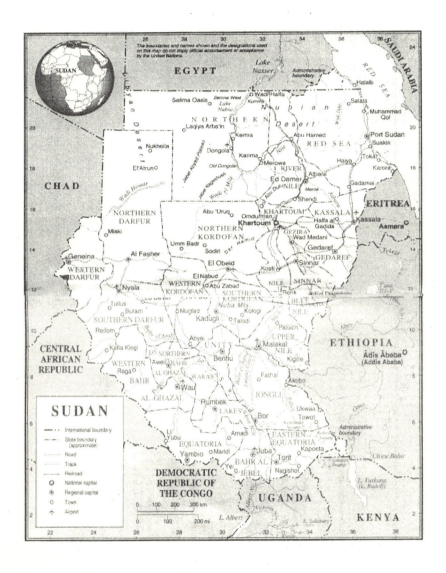

Abbreviations

AIDS	Acquired Immune Deficiency Syndrome
ANC	African National Congress (South Africa)
BBC	British Broadcasting Corporation
CCM	*Comitato Collaborazione Medica*
CIA	Central Intelligence Agency (US)
CPA	Comprehensive Peace Agreement
CRS	Catholic Relief Service (US)
EU	European Union
Frelimo	*Frente por la Liberatação de Moçambique*
IGAD	The Inter-Governmental Authority on Development
JMC	Joint Military Commission (of the SPLM/A-Sudan Government Peace Talks)
MM	Maryknoll Missionaries
NGO	Non-Governmental Organisation
NIF	National Islamic Front
NRRDO	Nuba Relief Rehabilitation and Development Organisation
NSCC	New Sudan Council of Churches
OLS	Operation Lifeline Sudan
PAIGC	*Partido Africana de Independencia de Guinea e Cabo Verde*
PPA	People for Peace in Africa
SCIO	Sudan Catholic Information Office
SJ	Society of Jesus
SPLM/A	Sudan Peoples Liberation Movement/Army
SRRA	Sudan Relief and Rehabilitation Association
SSIM	South Sudan Independence Movement
SSU	Sudan Socialist Party
UN	United Nations
UNDP	United Nations Development Fund
UNHCR	United Nations High Commissioner for Refugees
UNICEF	United Nations Children's Fund
US	United States (of America)
USCR	United States Committee for Refugees

Prologue

Father, I've heard about you. They say you often travel to Sudan. I know you've been to Leer… why don't you come to the Nuba Mountains? There are many Catholics there in need of a priest, and many boys in need of schools."

The speaker was Yousif Kuwa, sitting before me in my Kilimani Road office, Nairobi, early in January 1994. I no longer hoped in such a proposal, "Why don't you come to the Nuba Mountains?"

Kuwa, a Muslim, was the head of the SPLM (Sudan Peoples Liberation Movement) as well as a commander in the SPLA (Sudan Peoples Liberation Army), its military wing, for the Nuba Mountains. I was a missionary based in Nairobi, operating a youth community centre and in charge of a Catholic magazine. The Nuba people lived on the mountains made famous by Leni Riefenstahl. She had taken shots of their spectacular fights, painted bodies and colourful dances. She had been Hitler's photographer, and had been in search of the Nuba in imitation of George Rodger, another famous photographer. In the 1970s I had come across a book of Leni's photographs, and had developed a strong wish to know that rather heterogeneous nation and be a missionary in their midst.

The Nuba still bore in their flesh a long, and by no means concluded, history of slavery. They had succeeded in carving out for themselves an extraordinary habitat of mountain and hill tops, which is not usual on the continent. The reason was to escape the

9

slave-raiding caravans from El Obeid, capital of the Kordofan, which in the 1800s was an important slave market. Daniel Comboni, our founder, had himself dreamed of evangelising them personally. A few months before he died, in 1881, he went "to have a look at the Nuba people, ruined by slavery and 90% destroyed." Khartoum, where he penned those words, was the see of the huge Vicariate for Central Africa. The full report of that trip is lost, but in some of his letters Comboni spoke of the Nuba territory as a promising one: "Men and women go naked here as in Kic, but they look more vigorous and ready for evangelization."

The Nuba were the victims of a silent but real enough genocide, perpetrated for years. It was a cultural and genetic massacre taking place in the context of the longest African war. Following ferocious raids, the government enclosed the prisoners in so-called "peace camps." Men, women and children were mixed together after dismembering the family units, as a result of a *jihad* of Muslims against a largely Muslim people. It was a clear case of ethnic cleansing.

To get there on my own was a most difficult endeavour. But I couldn't say "no" to Yousif Kuwa after such a formal invitation. I began preparations.

Introduction

n the Nuba Mountains, war has ended. People move freely; in the markets one can find the essential commodities. As for the rest, almost two years after the signing of the peace treaty, it is becoming increasingly clear that the SPLA has abandoned us and we are the true losers of the peace treaty." The person talking to me prefers to remain unnamed. He belongs to the Nuba people and used to hold a prominent position in the Sudan People's Liberation Army but, some months ago, he chose exile. He says that he doesn't want to be part of a corrupt local government that has betrayed the promises of the long years of warfare. For years, this person has put his life at risk in the resistance against the Khartoum government but now that, at last, there is peace, he is in Nairobi and moves between the embassies of Western countries, in the hope of finding resettlement in one of them.

His disappointment is shared by many Nuba. The Nuba have contributed much to the SPLA cause. In the period from 1989 till 2002, thousands of their young men went to fight in the South, giving a very remarkable contribution to the resistance against the oppressive Khartoum government and to the building up of South Sudan. Moreover, for years, they have been a bulwark against the imposition of the Muslim fundamentalism coming from the North. Their position is strategically important geographically – being in the North but close to the South – and from the political and religious points of view because they are a people, for the majority, Islamized and yet who have been resisting the imposition of Islam and of Sharia'h Law. They are a fiercely independent people and do not accept orders from anybody, even from their co-faithful. This made them the subject of cruel government repressions, the last of which was the attack unleashed in May 2001.

But to understand the Nuba, we have to put their struggle in the context of the history of their country, the Sudan. The roots of the conflict are profound, going deep into the cultural, social, political and religious differences between the North and the South. On one side stand the peoples of the North, who consider themselves "Arabs", even though in reality they were arabised in relatively recent times, and who constitute roughly two thirds of the total population of the country. On the other side, in the South, there are peoples of nilotic origin, with cultures and languages strictly linked with Black Africa. These two great human groups have been in conflict for centuries, one of the causes of the conflict being slavery, mainly practiced by the North against the South. Yet the British colonialists put them together in a country called Sudan.

The first phase of the Sudan civil war started on 18 August 1955, a few months before independence, which came on 1 January 1956. It was a very low intensity war, and the rebels did not succeed to control any significant area or establish a separate administration. It was concluded in 1972, with the Addis Ababa Agreement, and followed by a period of broken promises by the Khartoum Government, so that the southerners felt there was no other alternative that to restart the war. Which happened in May 1983, under the banner of SPLM/A, an armed movement born, in the spirit of those days, as Marxist-Leninist and supported by USSR, China and Cuba. In a slow change of alliances, after 1989 the SPLA, and in particular its leader John Garang, became a faithful ally of the Americans, who already in the mid-nineties, used the SPLA as a barrier to control the Arabo Islamic expansionism. In this process the United States gave to Garang blind economic and military support in spite of the very undemocratic practices, to say the least, going on inside the movement, therefore fostering a dictatorial drift.

When the peace talks started in mid 2004, the two parties claiming to represent the North and the South had no clear mandate. In Khartoum Omar el Bashir, had seized power with a coup d'etat in 1989, suppressing every opposition, and in the South the strict control of Garang and his Dinka people had successfully made impossible to hear any dissenting voice. I believe that one of the reasons why the two parties were so reluctant to sit around a negotiation table, was precisely the fact that both were aware of their scant popular support, and that in the event of the implementation of truly free and fair election, this could come to light.

In this intricate situation, with military and political leaders that had switched allegiances several times, and a heavy external interference for making peace, any kind of peace, fast, other factors contributed in complicating the general picture.

Firstly, in September 1999 the Khartoum government succeeded in putting into exploitation – with the support of Chinese and Canadian companies – a number of oil wells geographically situated in the South but that have always been firmly in its hands. The income from these wells has put in the hands of the government a wealth that has changed the nature of the civil war, allowing it to buy weapons in quantities and qualities that it could never afford before.

Secondly, after 9/11, to avoid the danger of being listed as a rogue state, the Sudan government tried to appease the United States choosing a line of very cautious collaboration, giving out information on the Islamic extremists that had used Sudan as a base in the early nineties, and finally agreeing to peace talks, under the eager and vigilant supervision of the Americans.

Thirdly, as Khartoum's attitude became softer, in the United States the "religious right", having one of their own as President, became harder and bolder in demanding action against Khartoum. They started a campaign that, if it had the merit of keeping the international attention focused on Sudan, it has a visceral and unreasonable anti-Islamic attitude that has contributed in making people perceive the Sudan civil war as a religious war (I do not believe this to be true. I believe that the root cause of the Sudan civil war is lack of basic human rights for the Southerners), and has exacerbated the conflict, undermining the possibility of a religious peaceful coexistence for many years to come.

And why has the Bush administration wanted peace at any cost in Sudan, forcing, literally under duress, the two parties to sit around a negotiating table? The idea was that an American sponsored peace in Sudan would enormously enhance American prestige in this part of Africa, defuse the terrorism threat, create economic opportunities for the United States in the area, and show to the world that America could be a peace maker, not only a war wager. Unfortunately, as it has happened so many times with United States initiatives in this part of the world even when moved by the best intentions, the vision was not matched by a deep understanding of the situation on the ground, and things went awry.

In all these intricacies – and we have not even mentioned the interests of the countries bordering Sudan, another cause of complications – the peace process seemed to have lost the fundamental reason of the civil war, that is the vindication of the basic human rights by the non-Arabized peoples. Now, almost two years after the signing of the Comprehensive Peace Agreement in Nairobi on January 9 2005, the risk is that a peace, imposed from on high on two parties that did not fully represent the people, has not answered the legitimate demands of the people who have fought and given their lives for their homeland.

In this picture, the Nuba have always counted little within the liberation movement, notwithstanding their undisputed faithfulness to the SPLM/A. The SPLM/A revived the Nuba issue when it wanted to slow down or block negotiations with the Khartoum government, because it knew that the government was not ready to put into question the belonging of the Nuba to the North of the Sudan. But apart from these few moments of notoriety, the Nuba were always marginalized even within the SPLM/A.

It was, therefore, a big surprise when, in January 2002, the Nuba representatives, apparently with the mandate of the SPLA leadership, signed a ceasefire with the Khartoum government. Suddenly the Nuba became the experimentation field of a possible peace, and politically their cause became central in the dispute about the Sudanese civil war. But it didn't last long. The ceasefire in the Nuba Mountains, as it became clear in May of the same year, was only the first step to start the peace process imposed on both sides by the international community, in particular the US. Once more, the Nuba had been used as an experimental field, or as bait.

In the bulletin published at the end of the first round of the peace negotiations, which took place at Machakos (Kenya) in mid 2004, the situation of the Nuba Mountains and the "twin" area – the Southern Blue Nile – was not even mentioned. In those days the impression was that peace was going to be attained in a few weeks time. Instead, the peace agreement was reluctantly signed by both parties only in January 2005, also because the SPLA, which in July 2002 was not yet ready for peace, once more, as a way to slow down the negotiation, rediscovered the Nuba issue and for a few months made it central to the whole question of peace.

But again, with the increasing pressure for the peace treaty to be signed, the Nuba cause was sidestepped. The Comprehensive Peace Agreement (CPA) of January 9, 2005, although foreseeing "autonomy" for the Nuba, the terms of which are not specified, inserts them into the North without the possibility of a choice. They will not be allowed to take part in the referendum about the choice to remain united with the North or to separate. In the CPA, there is the possibility for the local Nuba parliament to pass laws with autonomy about topics that do not touch the general principles of the Constitution, about local items of minor importance, but the terms are not specified as well as the mandate of the vague "popular consultations" that are supposed to ratify these changes.

Was it worthwhile to undergo persecutions, to become the target of a real genocide, to lose thousands of lives defending the rights of the South in order to get so little? "Nothing, even" as the person who speaks with me specifies. At the moment, the Nuba are still savouring the relief of peace, with its unquestionable advantages, but the dissatisfaction is already creeping in, the more everybody realizes that peace will not allow the Nuba any form of self-determination. It is a morsel difficult to swallow by those who have set up a resistance that has had a terrible cost in terms of sacrifices and lost of human lives.

If one broadens the view to the whole of Sudan, the fear is that the forces that unleashed the civil war more than twenty years ago, and those responsible for the clashes in Darfur since the end of 2002, may not be able to control the consequences of the war they have fuelled, and that we might have to witness the progressive fragmentation of this largest country of Africa.

Yes, Darfur. Is it just coincidence that the clashes in Darfur started a few months after the beginning of the peace negotiations in Kenya? Previously this was a sleepy area that the SPLM/A had unsuccessfully tried to mobilize against the goverment. What has happended that has changed the situation so dramatically? Is it true that Darfur has enormous potential for oil? Who has sold or donated the weapons to the rebels? Who is supporting them? Chad? No jokes, please. Certainly the present Khartoum government – including the SPLM/A – is deeply responsible for what is happineg there. But somebody else is responsibile and we will not know who to blame unless we get the answers to the above questions.

In the meantime, in the South, the episodes of inter-ethnic violence continue; and in the East, among the Beja, everybody feels the threat of intensifying clashes. Only in Khartoum, Kosti, El Obeid, Port Sudan, the central government is firmly in control of the situation and is implementing development plans with alacrity. In the South, the almost total absence of cadres able to manage a new state, as well as the absence of a true leadership and a shared vision about the future of the whole area, seems to prepare the nightmare of a state in which programmes are planned and implemented by big international NGOs, whereas the local government is inefficient and corrupt.

16

Those who have the future of the great country at heart, hope that the impending danger of progressive disintegration will be stopped by strong political actions that will re-affirm its unity. It is necessary to give content to peace, e.g. the dignity and respect for human rights, the overcoming of extreme poverty, the construction of schools and hospitals. It is an enormous task, but it is a task that everybody must undertake – the government, the civil society, the churches, the local and international NGOs – to avoid falling into an abyss.

Father Renato Kizito Sesana,
Comboni Missionary
Nairobi, 12 November 2006

Failed Attempts

French anthropologist Hugo d'Aybaury was one of the very few able to reach the Nuba Mountains after the war had started. He dubbed himself "ethnodetective," in charge of shooting anthropological documentaries on behalf of Peekaboo Pictures, a small London firm.

In 1993 he spent three weeks in the region, shooting on 16mm film. The only means of locomotion until 2002 were donkeys, camels, or on foot. His original idea was to shoot an anthropological documentary, but on witnessing so much destruction he ended up filming a political one. This is what he reported on the Paris paper *Libération*:

On the 24th December 1992 alone, 6 000 inhabitants of the town of Heiban were massacred. I was given a list of 90 villages razed to the ground, ranging from the 700 inhabitants of Tibera to the 10 000 of Omdureen. The military operations respond to the same pattern: the soldiers arrive at night in military convoys, surround the village, shell the houses, shoot the survivors, and then flatten the ruins with tanks. They regularly leave behind 400-700 corpses.

One of the pictures shows a Nuba hurled onto the embers of a burning church. Two stumps could be seen where the hands had been. It was an umpteenth show of the genocidal intent of the government.

Despite the documented atrocities, Hugo d'Aybaury's documentary is not a controversial pamphlet. It underscores the pride of this people in the title *The Right to be Nuba*.

I met Hugo in 1996. We planned together to retrace Riefenstahl's

Kau, a name including also the Nyaro, some 3-4000 people altogether. They live atop two hills at the extreme south of the Nuba Mountains, and therefore isolated from the rest of the Nuba and close to the Shilluk, one of the main ethnic groups of South Sudan. Whenever I sought information about them, from the Nuba of Lomon for instance, the reaction was, "But they are backward people, they are primitive!"

Our hopes to visit the Kau-Nyaro rested on two pieces of information. The first was Hugo's friend Oswald Iten's, the second mine. Iten spent the whole of 1982 at Fungor, Kau and Nyaro, before the resumption of the North-South war, and shot an anthropological documentary. He had drafted a most accurate map of the villages, taking down the names of the heads of families, the number of cattle and even of fowl, everything. After gathering from him the necessary information, d'Aybaury had come to see me in Nairobi, knowing of my acquaintance with Lam Akol, the commander of the SPLA in Shilluk country. The most logical route to approach the zone was in fact from the south. We could count on hitching an air ride from CCM, a medical NGO from Turin, which every now and then sent an aircraft from Kenya to Aburok, 120km south of Fungor. From there perhaps we could proceed to Kau by car.

The idea proved impossible. Iten had in the meantime managed to reach Oriny in the company of Dr Joseph Meo of the CCM. There he traced some of the children that had appeared in his 1982 anthropological documentary. They entreated him not to proceed to Kau, least of all by car, so as not to provoke the locals into unpleasant reactions. "Shortly after you left Kau," they explained, "the village was attacked by the Dinka,[1] who killed the young men and raped the women. Eventually we repulsed them." From then on, anyone coming from the south was no longer welcome.

Abdelaziz Adam a-Hilu, successor of Kuwa at the head of the Nuba SPLM/A has other ideas as to what may have happened on that occasion. I think he is more credible, despite his partisan view, because he does not try to push it at all costs. He said,

[1]   The Dinka militated in the SPLA (author).

I know the Kau by direct experience. They are true Nuba, the last to remain untouched by Arab influence. The government may have organized that raid, although I don't know it for certain. But in any case that was the beginning of hostile feelings between the Kau and the SPLA. Cattle were raided, houses were burned and people killed. What is certain is that the government succeeded in deceiving them by spreading the rumour that Kuwa had organised that operation, despite the fact that at the time Kuwa had no military training despite having joined the Movement. I can assure you that no Nuba took part in that episode of violence. And Yousif is well known for not tolerating any abuse by his troops. He always punishes such things.

I also know the Kau-Nyaro personally. I met 60 of them in Eastern Sudan in 1997, as seasonal harvesters of durra, our staple crop. I tried to convince them to join us. Only four agreed, but for a very short time. Then they deserted and were not seen again. When they were with us I asked why they were so suspicious towards us. "Because Yousif came to loot and kill," they unhesitatingly replied. I tried to explain why it could not have been true, but they were stuck with the idea. And this explains why all in Kau are Muslims. In 2002 a person, very interested in what was happening in Kau gave me photos of the area taken before and after the conversion to Islam. The more recent photos showed hundreds of praying people wearing the *jallabia*, the traditional Arab robe.... It is a real pity, above all knowing Yousif's efforts to maintain Nuba culture and traditions.

In March 1995 I had the first opportunity to travel to the Nuba Mountains. I had been ordained priest on 18th March 1970, and naive as I was I thought I could celebrate my silver jubilee among them. But two days before my departure, a message from Kuwa, just back from the area, intimated me to stay where I was. A battle was raging next to the airstrip. There was nothing doing.

The second attempt took place in May. I had convinced Dr Meo to accompany me, so as to scout the area for ways of helping the Nuba medically. The plan contemplated my stopping at Pariang, where Meo and Dr Hashim Ziyada had taken a week to open a dispensary, collecting them and proceeding together.

At Lokichoggio I was ready to take off, when the aircraft suffered a breakdown. Finally we took off on 28th May on an old DC-3. In sight of Pariang we spotted smoke and fire from the ground, but we landed anyway. The local SPLA commander ordered us to leave at once.

"Why? We have come to pick up Dr Meo. Dr Meo comes tomorrow. Tomorrow?! He radioed us yesterday saying he would be here today!"

The commander ordered the wounded on board, ordering us at gunpoint to return to Lokichoggio. During the flight a soldier confided:

"The commander told me to tell you that Dr Meo has been taken prisoner."

The battle had concluded half an hour before our arrival. The zone was no man's land between the SPLA and Government forces. The latter had captured the two doctors, whose crime was to operate outside the approved area of OLS (Operation Lifeline Sudan) intervention. The OLS is the biggest humanitarian organization in the world. It was founded in 1989 following a tripartite agreement UN – Government – SPLA. It can act within the boundaries and the times agreed by the Khartoum Government and the UN. Outside those boundaries there is no salvation. The Nuba Mountains were outside those boundaries.

Back in Nairobi I informed the Italian embassy and the UN. Contacts and negotiations started at once. Dr Ziyada was introduced to the Italian public by the magazine *Famiglia Cristiana*:

He is the only Sudanese medical doctor in the whole area. A couple of years ago he was in the news for having been captured by the Government soldiers in the company of Dr Joseph Meo, with whom he had tried to assist medically the people of Pariang. They were released two months later. Dr Ziyada has since returned among his people, far from his family, which he has not seen for the past two years. He continues his humanitarian work, but clandestinely. "I am considered an enemy in my own country," as he puts it.

In June a BBC team succeeded in entering the Nuba Mountains. They stayed just the time for shooting *The Nuba: Sudan's Secret War* under the direction of Julie Flint, whom I met and appreciated. My turn came in August, together with three friends.

The Great "Quilombo" of Africa

Communities of fugitive African slaves were set up in colonial Brasil from the 16th to the 18th century by original deportees or their descendants. After managing to escape from sugar plantations or from the mines where they were prevalently employed, they sought refuge in faraway impervious and therefore impregnable zones. There they organized themselves into *mocambos*, villages where they cultivated maize, legumes, bananas, cassava and other crops. They organized themselves also politically, so as to defend themselves better. It is said that the systems they set up were highly democratic. A group of *mocambos* in a given territory formed a *quilombo*. The most famous of these was the Republic of Palmares. It lasted almost a century until its capitulation in 1695, following the killing of its leader Zumbi. In the Andes region the *quilombos* were called *palenques*. They were set up wherever a group of *cimarrones* (fugitive slaves) found among them a strong figure who could lead them.

On my first seeing them, the Nuba Mountains offered a scenario akin to that of the *quilombos*.

An accurate history of the Nuba people is yet to be written. The antecedents are not clear: they describe themselves as speaking 99 languages, as a kind of Africa within Africa. The most likely explanation is a series of migrations from the west, roughly today's Chad, to the east, at times in big groups, at others in dribs and drabs. The process is still going on.

There are signs of a uniform civilization all across the Sahara, starting from the 5th to the 3rd millennium B.C., from the Atlantic to the Red Sea. The same cultural elements can be spotted all along this immense zone, which can be seen in rock paintings as much as in architecture and other symbols.

> The Sahara rock carvings and paintings show humans with animal heads, dances and great, fantastic animals. They are the same images we find in ancient Egypt, with its gods provided with animal heads and its priests wearing masks like those found in the rock paintings. But we find the same symbols among today's African peoples, in the sacred masks of the Bambara, Cabre, Senufo, and the whole of the Fouta Djalon, and also in the sacred dances of the Bijagos of Guinea-Bissau. Let us not forget the big horns of the herds found in Egypt and Nubia, symbol of a solar cult, to be found to this day among the peoples of the Upper White Nile like the Shilluk, the Dinka and the Bari.[2]

The peopling of the Nuba Mountains took place against the same backdrop of constant migrations. A recent group of immigrants, the Noba or Nobati, came from the interior of the Sahel, settling partly in Southern Kordofan and partly between Khartoum and the first cataract of the Nile, up river from Aswan.

In the 4th century A.D. the Noba travelling eastward, away from the Sahel, reached the Nile and overthrew the Kushite kingdom of Meröe, the ruins of which are still visible near Bajrawiya north of Khartoum. Why the Kushite kingdom was declining is not clear: In the 7th century B.C. there had been Kushite Pharaohs on the throne of Egypt. In the 6th-7th centuries A.D. Lower and Upper Nubia were evangelized. The territory stretched from Egypt south of the first cataract to Sudan north of the sixth one. Three Christian kingdoms rose: Nobat, Makuria and Aloa. But following the onslaught of Islam the three kingdoms began to crumble. Between the 13th and 14th century many Nubians sought refuge southwards, and settled on what are today the Nuba Mountains. Whether the mountains were named after them or after the Noba who were already there, is not clear at all.

There are undoubted connections between ancient Nubia and Nuba country, but they account for a very minor part of the history

[2]   Maurizio Damiano, *Nigrizia*.

of Southern Kordofan. Linguistically, only the Dair, Kadaru, Killing, Ghulfan and Karko, living on the north western hills, speak languages related to Nubian. Ronald Stevenson is the author of *The Nuba People of the Kordofan Province*, published in 1984. He gathered a huge quantity of data and expressed reasonable hypotheses, but warned his readers that no one could be in a position to say the last word on the ancient history of that area in the heart of Sudan. Effectively he was repeating what Siegfried Frederick Nadel had said some 40 years earlier: "We know little of Nuba ancient history."

The Austrian in the service of the British crown could not foresee, though, the impact that his 500-page volume would have on Yousif Kuwa, and through him on tens of thousands of his brethren. "The more I read, the more I recognized myself," he once told me. "From that moment on I began to look at my past, the world whence I came, no longer in spiteful terms as I had been taught, but positively." We shall see how much he learned from that reading.

If ancient history does not give much information about the origin, migrations and events regarding the Nuba, the chronicles of the past two centuries are documented enough to justify the image of a Nuba *quilombo* the size of Wales.

> Many Nuba were northern peoples, retreating from the north because of wars along the centuries, and coming to a mountainous country for better protection.

These are the words of Ngaiko Ramadan Orandi, who served as Kuwa's bodyguard for six years, a three-star captain as he describes himself. He later became the head of a primary school at Kujur Shabia, set up in SPLA-controlled area and sponsored by Koinonia.[3] Ramadan is also keen on the Tira culture of his people:

> The Tira are not indigenous. They used to live around Kadugli, towards Tiberi. They came here, SE of Heiban, during the Mahdi revolution towards the end of the 19th century. The Arabs were hunting them down to enslave them. They ran away and settled at Nagorban and in Rashad County.

³ Koinonia is a youth community, based in Nairobi, that aims at peace-building and intercultural exchange.

24

Ramadan's words confirm the data about successive migrations, superimposing themselves on pre-existing groups that did not inhabit crests and tops, but the fertile plains surrounding the mountains. The Nuba Mountains, in fact, are not mountains properly so-called, but a geographically varied country, spread between Southern and Western Kordofan. They consist of rocky hills rising up to 400m over the plains, alternating with valleys and plains. Inselbergs rise up here and there, together with isolated relief features including mountains with sheer cliffs. The highest peak does not attain 1500m of altitude. Wide plateaus are enclosed within the system. The mountains are true natural fortresses, pock-marked with caves for greater security. The caves open in steep slopes, and often give shelter to people seeking safety. Such a landscape was the theatre of many diverse stories along the centuries. Stevenson remarked: "Let's not assume that each and every one of these tribes undertook large-scale migrations."

Also, the new arrivals could have met already settled groups who had arrived so long before as to be considered "indigenous."

Let us now try to give an answer to the question "Who are the Nuba? Where do they come from?", in agreement with Canadian linguist Robin Thelwall. His opinion was published by the review *Nuba Survival* in February 2002. The review is the voice of Nuba intellectual circles headed by Suleiman Musa Rahhal. Thelwall maintains that

> The 50-odd languages spoken in Nubaland can be divided into two-three linguistic families, Nilo-Saharan and Kordofan, which is a sub-family of the Niger-Kordofan group. One must add also Arabic, which must have been introduced after the Islamic invasion of Egypt in the 7th century. Some small groups speak Fulani and other West African languages. All other languages are anterior to these, and have been there mostly from time immemorial.

On the Nuba Mountains the Heiban, Talodi, Rasha and Katla speak a Kordofan language. The names of the groups are based, as Thelwall points out,

> on geographical centres proposed by Thilo Schadeberg, different from those employed in the normal literature. The Kadugli group, formerly attributed to the Kordofan family, was removed by Schadeberg to the

Nilo-Saharan. Kordofan sub-groups are located in the south and east of the Nuba Mountains. The rest of the Nuba languages belong to the more important Nilo-Saharan subgroup called "East Sudanic." Other groups outside the Mountains are akin to these: some are Nilotic groups, plus stray groups like the Tama of Darfur, the Nera of Eritrea and the Jebel of the Upper Blue Nile.

The languages spoken by the "Hill Nubians" and by the Daju are the evident result of settlements of outsiders among the Nuba. Thelwall doubts that the Nubian language properly so called arrived there from Nubia proper. It is true, for instance, that the names of the days of the week originate from Christian Nubia; but all this indicates is that there were inter-lingual contacts "at least during the Christian Nubian period from the 6th to the 15th century." The "Hill Nubians" could simply

> have spread from central Kordofan towards the Nuba Mountains during Nubian political ascendancy from Aswan to Kosti, or even further south. In any case, given the location of the groups that speak Hill Nubian (Dair, Dilling, Karko, etc.) along the North-Eastern fringe of the mountains, it is clear that they are immigrants among the Nyima and the Temein.

The latter groups must have dwelt there for a long time. The last group, the Daju, includes no less than six dialects, scattered throughout the wide area that from the Kordofan goes towards Eastern Chad through Darfur. The Canadian linguist concludes:

> The only two groups present on the Nuba Mountains younger than 2000 years are the Lagawa Daju and the Hill Nubians. All the other languages, and therefore peoples, have been in the region probably longer than 2000 years.

Let us return to more recent documented history, tracing the forging of today's Nuba identity.

In 1772 James Bruce landed at Sennar on the Blue Nile, looking for the source of the river like many before and after him. He found groups of Nuba living around the capital of the Funj kingdom. They were Arabised, and forcibly recruited as soldiers from their ancestral land in the west. The army they were soldiering in belonged to a state that held power in the region for a long time: the Black Sultanate, which held sway up to the Kordofan.

26

On the occasion of my first journey in the area, I too saw the ruins of a palace that the locals averred to have belonged to a famous and cruel woman Sultan in the second half of the 19th century. She was still remembered as one who had determinedly resisted the British. Bruce wrote: "Many people I spoke to are Blacks of a gentler mien than the Funj of the Sennar kingdom." There are a good 14 000 of them, divided into small villages. They have curly hair and flat nose like the other Blacks. Their tongue is pleasing and sonorous, but radically different from all the ones I have heard."

The foregoing is the first European mention of the Nuba. In the last decade of the 18th century another European traveller, William George Browne, journeyed through Nuba territory. At Sheibun, south of the Kadugli-Heiban road, near Otoro, some merchants hailing from Dongola had started prospecting for gold. Browne noted the "great number" of slaves, but remarks that the Nuba

are independent tribes. Their only leaders are their chiefs, whose authority is minimal except in war time. The mek (Sultan) of Sennar used to receive tribute from the people of Sheibun, but for some time he has received nothing...

Stevenson noted instead that "Tegali paid his yearly tribute either in gold or in slaves."

The Baggara, herdsmen hailing from the north and west, became famous for their slave raids among the Nuba from 1800. In 1922, J. W. Sagar, quoted by Stevenson, described them as follows:

The slave raids began, and the Nuba were thrust on the hills. The agreed procedure was that every Baggara sub-tribe would protect the hills under its jurisdiction in exchange for grain and slaves, insofar as possible, and raided, insofar as possible, the hills protected by another sub-tribe. Cultivation in the plains ceased, for fear of sudden attacks by the formidable riders. The Nuba terraced the hills for seed and to stave off hunger. But the produce thus cultivated was of poor quality and often failed to mature. In the worst moments the Nuba found themselves forced to sell their children to the Arabs in exchange for food.

It was not always like that, or always to the same extent. I quote such texts because I think I can read in them the early motives for the 1985 war.

The 1821 conquest of Sudan by Egypt, in turn an Ottoman possession, institutionalized slave raids. Two years later the Viceroy Muhammad Ali, unhappy with the results of seasonal raids, wrote to the Governor of the Kordofan:

> You well know that our efforts are aimed at getting Blacks. *Please show your zeal in bringing our desires to fulfilment in this matter of capital importance.*

The "desires" were orders. If what the German Ignatius Pallme tells is true,

> Four years after the conquest, the number of slaves for the Viceroy in Egypt was estimated at 40 000; in 1839 it rose to 200 000, without reckoning the numbers captured by the Baggara and purchased by the *jallaba* merchants.

It is also true that in 1854 an order arrived from the new viceroy in Cairo. The European powers had decreed the end of slavery, and he ordered his governors to comply. But it was all show: when all was said and done the order had to be carried out by the local authorities. Josephine Bakhita, the first canonised Sudanese, was born 15 years after that royal edict: wrenched off her village in the Darfur when still a child, repeatedly bought and sold, was finally liberated by the Italian Consul at Khartoum and taken to Italy. She became a Canossian nun, and her memory is still very much alive in Schio, Upper Vicenza country. The story of Mende Nazer, virtually identical to Bakhita's, belongs to our days. She is a Karko, who told it in first person to a journalist, who published it at once.[4]

Luckily Ignatius Pallme has related lighter information, like that the Nuba are republican, in that they recognise the authority of the village chief, but are ready to vote on important issues. In his *Travels in Kordofan* Pallme listed the meagre domestic goods in their possession, like pots and double-edged knives, and produce for exchange with traders, like ostrich feathers, tamarind and honey (and slaves) against tobacco, salt and cowry shells.

The students of the schools in Kerker and Kujur Shabia have collected some Nuba legends, made use of in an anthology for the

[4]   *Schiava*, Sperling and Kupfer 2003.

learning of English. There are three stories purporting to give the etymology of as many Nuba groups: the Otoro, the Tira and the Lira. The version is in the form of myth, but not devoid of interest.

When Arab raiders looking for slaves hunted the Nuba in North Sudan, the Lira migrated south towards the Kordofan, and stopped near Kwalib. It happened so many years ago that not even the oldest among the Lira has personal memories of it. The Arabs continued chasing the Lira wherever they settled. Increasingly worried by the permanent threat, they killed a goat, and the receivers of the goat's entrails were the ones supposed to preserve the secrets of the tribe. They swore to keep the secrets till the end. In their language the entrails of an animal are called *lare*, hence their name.

For the Otoro too, the memory of slave raids is central.

Once upon a time the Otoro lived on Kilira Mountain. They cultivated the soil and raised cows, pigs, goats and sheep. Their lands were very fertile, and they always had abundant food. All the travellers were astonished at Otoro strength and valour. Some were happy to be their friends, others became their enemies. The Otoro kept a bull at the approach of the hill, which was supposed to give the alarm at enemy approach. One day the Arabs decided to go and raid the Otoro for slaves and cattle. They approached Mt Kilira and saw no sentry except the bull. They got excited at the prospect of a lightning raid and of escaping with rich loot. But as soon as they went beyond the bull, it mooed. They were thus repulsed and defeated. They repeated the experiment, with the same result. Thus did the Arab robbers begin to tell the story of a *thaur* (Arabic for bull) that incites the Kilira people to war. Since then the Arabs call the people of Kilira Mountain *thorawi*, or "people of the bull," or the "courageous people."

The Tira describe themselves, like the Lira, as having come from the northern areas of the Sudan. Famine and conflict chased them away from their ancestral lands onto the heights of the Kordofan (in Nubian *kordu* means man and *fan* land).

Some 2000 years ago there lived a girl called Tira. All people living in the Kaddar Kibbiri were attracted by her. One day some nomadic Arabs passed by and saw her. A few weeks later they returned and kidnapped her. From that day, Tira's people are called Tira after her. The name has remained.

29

A Missionary's Dream

D aniel Comboni, first bishop of Khartoum in charge of the immense Central African Vicariate, had a soft spot for the Nuba. He was able to travel within the *Gebel Nuba*, the Nuba Mountains, only in his 50th – and last – year of his life. Before that all he could do was to reach Dilling, the NW access to the area. In June 1881 he wanted to see everything, especially Karko, so as to found a small mission station in the Small Golfan. Among his fellow travellers was Alphonse Roversi, who shortly before had been named inspector for the suppression of the slave trade by the Governor General of the Sudan. Roversi had drawn a most accurate map of the *Dar Nuba* (Nubaland). Comboni added the information of this map to that drawn by the missionary Stanislaus Carcereri, thus improving it substantially. The General Report of that journey has been lost, on the assumption that Comboni actually wrote it in the three remaining months of his life before the fever took him.[5] There are traces of it here and there in his countless letters.

Comboni's soft spot for the Nuba was due to their being a favourite target of the slave raiders. Carcereri's warm diary must also have influenced him. But his favourable judgement was undoubtedly due to his having met some of them personally before undertaking that last journey.

---

[5] He said: "I will draft it when I get better, unless I die" realistically enough.

While in El Obeid, ready for the exploration, he had received a flattering letter from the Governor General Muhammad Rauf:

I would ask you, Monsignor, to examine the country and its administration with attention, so that we may take the necessary measures for the welfare of those peoples and provide for their prosperity.

What worried Pasha Rauf most was the question of slavery:

When on the ground, you will be able to uncover and get acquainted with the errors committed there, and propose a solution.

Comboni enjoyed a fearful reputation as a leader in the abolitionist struggle. He thought he could see results after his first intervention:

The joy and enthusiasm of those chiefs and their people are to be seen to be believed. After my visit they did not experience being robbed of sons, daughters, cows and goats, and unanimously acknowledge that it was the Catholic Church that liberated them. The more so when they saw the Baggara chiefs being arrested, as literally as I had promised they would be.

The three visits of a Nuba chief particularly impressed Comboni. He dreamt:

His name is Nemur. He lords it over a number of villages that have never agreed to pay tribute. He is in touch with almost all the chiefs or kings of the Nuba people that were never conquered by the Turks, and are still independent. This king *explicitly invited me* to visit his country, establish schools and teach them our religion.

The emphasis is Comboni's. Next came the visit of a *kujur*:

In September the chief of the Nuba could not come to El Obeid. But he sent on his behalf the *Kujur* of the Nuba, a kind of priest-doctor-magician called in their language Oek. He has more authority than the chiefs themselves. He spent three hours with me, visiting our church, the workshop, the tools used in carpentry, shoemaking, blacksmithing, and farming. He was shown photographs and heard the sound of the accordion and harmonium that I played for him. Boys that had shortly before been abducted and rescued, some Nuba among them, sang for him. The great magician and his retinue were astonished and full of admiration. He entreated me warmly to set up a mission in his country and to travel there in haste, promising that we would be welcome as their fathers and brothers.

31

The first girl to take the veil for the Institute of the *Pie Madri della Nigrizia,* founded by Comboni, was a Nuba, 18-year old Fortunata Kwashe "born at Tongojo, 10° north in the Nuba Mountains. She too, like many others, had been abducted as a young girl, and rescued by Fr Jeremiah of Leghorn, a Franciscan, in Cairo.

But what inclined Comboni more than anything else was the friendship struck in Verona, at the age of 18, when studying at the Mazza Institute, with an excellent young Black man, liberated from slavery and adopted by the Miniscalchi family. His name was Bakhit Kaenda, of the Jebel Nuba tribe, who greatly impressed Comboni.

> I struck a strong friendship with this African, a most fervent Catholic. I developed a strong interest for his native country. With me, also most Catholic Verona was full of admiration for this Nuba of strong faith and refined piety. To these qualities he added a redoubtable character. Through him I formed a high opinion of the Nuba, and repeated to him often: "I will not rest until I have planted the Cross of Christ in your land. During the first years of my ministry the thing was impossible, because the apostolate of the missionaries in Central Africa was restricted to the White Nile. But when I arrived in the Kordofan as Administrator of the territory and daily heard stories about Nubaland, about the fidelity and courage of the Nuba slaves streaming through El Obeid, my heart grew eager again to bring the light of the Faith to them.

In 1873 he sent an advance party of collaborators, to feel the ground and choose a spot for the first Mission station in Dar Nuba. The place chosen was Dilling (or Delen).

> The advance party I sent under Fr Carcereri to Nubaland was received with maximum enthusiasm by the great magician and by the inhabitants. They offered the visitors anything they wished: land, houses, even the chief's residence. They asked for them to stay for good.

Comboni's enthusiasm knew no bounds:

> The Nuba Mission shows advantages far superior to any other attempt made by the Church in central Africa. No European ever penetrated there, Islam did not strike any root, and no commercial establishment was ever set up.

Fr Carcereri corroborates, after his first visit to the territory, which entailed crossing Baggara lands. The missionary declares himself happy not to have accepted an escort of 200 men he had been offered.

The Baggara, just like the Blacks, are suspicious of anyone who does not trust them. But if they sense trust in the foreigner, they are the most peaceful and hospitable people in the world.

He happened to meet a group of mounted Baggara face to face, as they were at full gallop armed with firearms, spears and shields. They ended up drinking coffee and camping together for the night. Later Fr Stanislaus learned that they were going to raid for slaves the poor people of a village above Golfan.

Like most 19th century Italian missionaries, Carcereri was a very keen observer.

It is as if nature came to the defence of those poor inhabitants of the mountains. The ground is thick with Mimosa with very sharp thorns like the Hharag bushes.

Kujur Kakum, the same who had visited the El Obeid mission shortly before, came down to meet him. Carcereri waxes lyrical about the democratic sentiments of the Nuba, where authority is managed in close contact with the people, unlike Europe:

He calls to war by playing the war drums. He decides all disputes between his subjects. No decision is taken, or affairs concluded, without him. He would err who judged among these people the same formalities and protocol that among us separate the sovereign from his subjects. The King of Delen has none of that. He is like the father of a family, like the ancient patriarch, accessible to all. He even earns his bread by working, like everybody else. He does not impose taxes, has no courts of law, and no bodyguards or guards of honour. There is no standing army. He wears some insignia of office, as I will explain, but these appear on great occasions, and no more. The Kujur greeted us embracing and kissing us: the others shook our hands and the youth expected us to touch their right shoulder and arm.

The triumphal entry into Delen was greeted with volleys of gunfire, shouts, clapping of hands, games and horse races. The day ended in the "royal residence" of the Kujur, half way up the slope of the fourth of the five mountains making up Jebel Delen, a gigantic block of stone. In a spacious and treed opening there were five round mud huts *(dordor)* and a wooden one covered with straw *(tokol)*. The *dordor* are

> round or square rooms built with compacted soil mixed with gravel, impervious to rain and covered with a conical thatched roof. The tokol is like the *dordor*, but entirely made of straw around a framework of ebony.

Carcereri's account goes on explaining the canons of Nuba building, which have not changed much in a century. Every *dordor* has a single use: one for the parents' bedroom, another for the children, for guests, for the kitchen, etc. Even Yousif Kuwa's mausoleum, in Luere, was built with that style. The novelty is that one of the rooms has been set aside for his library.

Fr Stanislaus noted, in the area he was able to visit during his two weeks there, a great variety of building types.

> Their huts have the most curiously varied shapes: square, round, pentagonal, hexagonal, oblong, and others long and narrow like a wine barrel. Let me add that every nook and cranny is being used as a store, including natural caves and cracks in the mountain itself.

A university student who accompanied me to the Nuba Mountains, wrote his dissertation thesis in civil engineering on the basis of his observations of Nuba building standards. They also had, in the account of our missionary,

> built cisterns and dug wells in the lower slopes, which afford them sufficient water for all their needs.

Comboni's envoys experienced a first-rate hospitality. They were received under a tent erected in front of a house.

> At once the *angareb* were set up; then they served a most refreshing drink of water and honey, pastry, black *durra* cane as sweet as sugar cane; then an *assida* of red *maregh*, mutton, chicken, abundant milk and honey, and even a *dokhon* cake made of honey, butter and eggs. All the servants and women of the *Kujur* were constantly busy to satisfy his generosity towards us.

He goes on explaining the terms used: the *angareb* was a kind of small sofa doubling up as bed, in common use throughout the Sudan. It is made of hard wood, and the pieces are kept together by lashings from animal skins. Similar furniture was found in the tombs of the Pharaohs, only more sumptuous. Today the "bedspring" is made of vegetable fibre.

The *assida* is a maize meal of some consistency. After grinding the grains between two smooth granite stones, the flour is mixed with warm water, and cooked over a low fire while continuously stirring.[6]

Durra, maregh and *dokhon* are varieties of cereals. The *durra*, or sorghum, is the staple food.

The traveller now touches a sorry point:

> On those mountains then, there dwell a large but unhappy people, forced there by the inhuman *Jalaba* intent on kidnapping their children. Once upon a time they inhabited the valley below, and counterattacked their aggressors with arrows and spears; but as soon as the Sudan got flooded with firearms, which were beyond their reach, their traditional weapons could not repulse the attacks, and had to withdraw, vying with hyenas and tigers [sic] for shelter. The cattle climb up with them in the evenings, while their crops remain exposed in the valley below to the raids of the greedy Baggara.

The sympathy of the missionary for the Nuba does not extend to their religion, in which "everything is reduced to practices akin to magic, as far as I could understand."

This was the "darkness" which 19th century missionaries had come to dispel. But there was something positive in the matter of religion:

> They are absolutely immune to Islam. They have a rite, at the birth of a child, which looks like a shadow, a languid memory of the Christian baptism.

By "memory" Fr Stanislaus betrays his view that the Nuba descended from the Nubian Christians, who in turn had for ancestor in the faith the eunuch of the Kandaké of Acts 8:26-40. The Kandaké resided in Napete, later Datba and today Debba, between the two Nubias. He warmly recommended a missionary foundation among them, since they had

> a genuine and sincere character, very intelligent. Their complexion is strong and frank, and their intelligence calls for a matching education.

[6] In the Nuba villages one finds basalt blocks hollowed by such grinding action over decades.

35

They asked for the explanation of everything they saw or heard from us. They easily understood, and immediately taught others. They are industrious and hard workers. Like other Africans, the Nuba are also polygamous, but many, either by choice or by necessity have only one woman. Their lifestyle is sober. They do not drink alcohol except on solemnities. For minor celebrations they drink *merissa,* a kind of beer of fermented *dokhon.*

Some two years later Comboni went to Delen. He related the extraordinary welcome reserved to him, and felt confirmed in his expectations about that people,

Without any doubt the most intelligent of all tribes and races visited by me during the past 18 years in Central Africa. But we ought to overcome many a superstition, and convince them to wear clothes. Out of every hundred men hardly one wears a rag or a skin over the parts of the body that ought to be covered. Among women it is worse still; for every one that wears a little cotton, there are 200 that don't even wear that. Hence the usefulness of Sisters who may educate these black women. Cotton grows here, and with it dresses can be made to provide better garments for these people.

Comboni knew that women went around naked because of the superstition according to which clothes prevented them from bearing children. The Sisters arrived at the end of the 1880s. Michelangelo Grancelli, Comboni's first biographer, writes:

The first Pious Mothers: Sisters Eulalia Pesavento, Maria Caprini and Teresa Grigolini arrived at the Jebel Nuba from El Obeid after four days on camel back.

They were the first white women to reach the Nuba Mountains.

However "primitive" the Nuba might have appeared to Comboni, he thought very highly of them, especially because of their hard working habits.

They work much harder than the tribes on the White Nile, and cultivate their land so as to make it give crops the year around. Furthermore, they show intelligence and judgement. Speaking to them one has often the impression of speaking to a cultured European; also, they have a fine sense of duty and great respect for the priesthood. Another good point is that they are very united, they help each other and when a common danger threatens they do not hesitate in risking their lives. Hardly ever do internal quarrels arise among them. Their life is almost patriarchal. The Nuba are one of the most interesting and likeable races of Central Africa.

Comboni, like Carcereri and Pallme, also admired their democratic spirit:

> They have no law, no written code, and no violence; their chief governs most pacifically. All have recourse to him for the slightest lawsuits, obey his judgement, and the guilty accept whatever punishment he metes out. Nevertheless the chief does not undertake any important course of action without consulting the elders. They all sit under a baobab tree and tackle the smallest issues with such maturity as to cause wonder. I myself witnessed such meetings several times.

In a letter to his father he related having brought to completion

> a difficult but necessary exploration over more than 50 mountains, on horseback or on foot, sleeping on mats, eating insipid food, and under the burden of many privations; but when one works for Jesus everything tastes sweet. We had climbed Mt. Karkendi under a blistering, suffocating sun. I had left my horse down below to the care of the six Turkish guards. They asked us to sit down on some knotty poles in the shade, surrounded by an enormous throng of blacks big and small, and of women young and old, all of them wearing the fashion of our first parents Adam and Eve before they foolishly sinned.

Still writing to his father, he reveals his obsession with the issue of slavery, realistically enough about the means and optimistically about the outcome of the struggle.

> I drafted a plan for the Sudanese government to uproot the slave trading of the Nuba, who are decimated year in year out. The chiefs, Kujurs and Sultans threw themselves at my feet, begging to be liberated from this scourge. From 1838, when Bakhit Miniscalchi was abducted, to date, the population was almost destroyed, reduced to 1/15 of its former strength. I will succeed, because I have the support of the government. Furthermore, a French captain with a troop of soldiers lodges in our house in Delen, with orders to consult me. After the first skirmish, a Baggara chief was killed and another captured. They belong to the group that had abducted Bakhit. Terror has now spread among these murderous brigands, who are no longer protected by the government. In six months the end of the slave trade will be an accomplished fact, to the greater honour of the Church and of the Mission that was its first and strongest instrument, to the greater glory of God and the good of this unhappy people.

Identities

In the very days when Comboni was wandering around the Nuba heights, Muhammad Ahmad bin Abdallah launched his religious appeal from Kosti, a small islet on the White Nile. The self-styled "Mahdi" was calling for independence from Egyptian-Turkish domination. The Islamic Messiah's Holy War raged here and there in the whole of the Sudan.

The Mahdi died in 1885, after having taken Khartoum by storm and killed Gordon Pasha. The Khalifa Abdullahi succeeded him, setting up a theocratic state with rather stormy internal vicissitudes until 1898. The Egyptians re-conquered the Sudan with decisive British help. They excogitated the peculiar solution called "Anglo-Egyptian Sudan" that held until independence in 1956. The war 1985-2005 has its origin in these past events.

What did the Mahdi rebellion mean for the Nuba? The key event is the pact stipulated by the Mahdi with Adam Dabbalu, sovereign of Tegali. The Tegali kingdom, located at the extreme NE of Nubaland, was the most organized of the Nuba polities, with accurate historical records going back to the 13th century. It was in good relations with the Funj kingdom of Sennar. With the pact, Dabalu attempted a third way between an all-out alliance with the Mahdi and an all-out resistance. His counsellors did not agree to it, judging the Mahdi "an impostor." They were right. Adam Dabbalu was "invited" to El Obeid and detained there, where he died shortly

38

afterwards. An all-out attack followed on the Tegali kingdom, which was brought to an end.

Various Nuba peoples struck an alliance with the Mahdi. Only the Dair opposed him strenuously. Josef Ohrwalder, a Comboni missionary residing in Dilling, wrote in his diary:

Mt. Dobab, called Deir by the Arabs for its semicircular shape, is a mountain in Nubaland in the shape of a natural fortress. It is accessible only from one side, where defence is rather easy. There are many water points, so that it can withstand a long siege. The Mahdi had his sights trained on *Jebel Nuba*.[7] Abu Anjia and other emirs had repeatedly failed in their assaults, which had all been repulsed. The Mahdi sent all his fighters to Deir, encouraging them to exercise themselves in the holy war and to do penance for having adhered to his cause so late. War against the Nuba was waged with maximum cruelty. The proud Fogara were furious at those miserable slaves, as they called the Nuba, who resisted them so obstinately. In one of the assaults the Fogara set on fire the huts of the Nuba, killed many men and sent women and children to Rahad to be sold into slavery. Angher beheaded three Nuba who had surrendered, and Abu Anjia's soldiers grabbed little children by their feet and smashed their heads against the rocks. In Rahad they had a *zeriba* (fence) built to keep the Nuba prisoners.

Such methods were the forerunners of the "peace camps" of the 1990s. Ohrwalder goes on relating how the Baggara operated. From their centre at Sinjakai, some six hours from Delen in the north, they moved in groups of 150-200 men on horseback, raiding the mountain slopes. They attacked all of a sudden and retreated equally fast. Anything found on the way they either destroyed or took away. Their favourite targets were Nuba farmers at work in the fields and women fetching water at the wells.

The Nuba fought with desperate courage, but the Fogara forces were overwhelming, so much so that the Nuba surrendered on condition of being left free to continue living on their mountain. Peace seemed to return. The Mahdi released many Dair prisoners. But on sensing that they were about to be deported towards the White Nile,

---

[7] Arabic for Nuba Mountains.

the Nuba ran away during the night and agreed that they would rather die of hunger than abandon their land. They went up their mountain again and war resumed. The Nuba suffered many casualties, but so did the Fogara. The Nuba retreated to places inaccessible to the Fogara, who got tired of useless fighting and gave up.

When trying to cross the wadi Chor Hobil, swollen by the 1884 rains, they perished in the flash flood by the hundreds.

A period of tranquillity ensued. The chronicles are full of raids and clashes down to Talodi, south of the Nuba Mountains, with the Baggara and legions of new slaves on stage again.

Father Ohrwalder relates a story very much akin to the Brasilian *quilombos*. A few hundred black soldiers, recruited by the Turkish-Egyptian administration and later forcibly incorporated among the *jihadiyya*, the Mahdi's Rifles, mutinied in September 1885. Joined by a throng of slaves, they made their way to the Nuba Mountains from El Obeid. They were quartered at Ghulfan, on an almost inaccessible mountain, where they set up some kind of military republic after declaring the Mahdia overthrown. They set up a government at Dilling, headed by a certain Bashir. Then they fought against the local Nyima, one of the Nuba tribes.

Months later the *quilombolas* repulsed a Mahdist attack and resisted for another year, after which they were routed. It was 1886. The contemporary Egyptian Intelligence Report relates that as late as 1894 there still operated a resistance nucleus on the Nuba Mountains, led by a certain Somit. They had often overpowered the dervishes and offered asylum to all the Black *Jihadiyya* unhappy under dervish authority. By "dervish" is meant the *ansar*, the soldiers of the Mahdi, who was himself a dervish, i.e. a Sufi mystic. In fact the Sufi were warriors, who more often than not attained great economic and military power.

The first years under the Anglo-Egyptian condominium were more peaceful than the 20-year period under the Mahdi, but not fully exempt from action. The spreading of firearms, between those captured from the enemy and those brought home by the *jihadiyya* veterans, destabilised the country with intertribal clashes. The Nuba groups, relying on past experience, took various stands in the face of the new white power: some conformed, others resisted. The government was forced to patrol the area as best it could, while studying and restudying the administrative arrangement of the area. British doctrine about *indirect rule*, i.e. governing by means of native chiefs, was applied in the Sudan in the 1920s. It reached the Nuba Mountains with delayed action: in a society without centralised power, the colonial administration had to invent, and impose, chiefs. The policy adopted for the Blue Nile and the Nuba Mountains, geographically in the north but culturally southern, was that of the "closed districts." Freedom of circulation between north and south was severely limited, with the view of facilitating the final abolition of slavery and stopping Islamic expansion in non-Islamised districts. Even this arrangement would be at the root of the many civil wars plaguing the Sudan.

Its consequences are felt to this day. The Nuba were denied access to education and development, whereas the northern Arabs found themselves in a privileged position. From the positive side, security improved. No one was allowed into Nuba territory, whereas the Nuba were free to travel to El Obeid and Khartoum. Many who got city jobs as servants in Arab homes, with the most menial occupations, went back home converted to Islam, thus contributing to its expansion. Islam, Africanised and integrated with local tradition, has thus become the religion of about half the Nuba population. Christianity too expanded thanks to returning migrants.

The closed district policy has had also long term political consequences, with a bearing on war and peace negotiations. To a journalist who asked Yousif Kuwa whether the Nuba Mountains and the southern Blue Nile should be considered part of the South, he answered:

> Yes. Historically, it is more correct to go back to the 1922 British administrative decision rather than the post-independence one. President Omar Bashir's insistence on the 1956 forced annexation of the two territories to the North is the root of all problems. The secession of the South, but without the Blue Nile and the Nuba Mountains allows him

to get his troops ready and concentrate them in the two zones left out of the agreement. Let us not forget that the Khartoum government's intention is to expand Islam to the whole world. Any declaration, however innocuous-sounding, has to be interpreted in this context. That's why we refuse to separate "the southern question" from the "Nuba-Blue Nile" question.

"The name 'Nuba' has been given to all the Blacks hailing from slave-country south of the Sennar," wrote the Swiss explorer Johann Ludwing Burckhardt in 1819. It was a name given indiscriminately to a heterogeneous group of people by those who took them to be no more than black gold, i.e. slaves. And so "Nuba" became their first declaration of identity. Only the Tegali insist in calling themselves "Tegali." The urbanized Shawabna, of mixed origin and educated, also insist on their aboriginal name: to be called "Nuba" is certainly not a status symbol among them. Such an identity is a mark of oppression and marginalization. I remember the first Nuba I met in Nairobi. I had sent for them to come to the Koinonia community near the Kivuli centre, where street children were catered for. There must have been 30 or 40 of them. They were astonished: "Who would care for the Nuba? Why did Fr Kizito call us here?" They still feel the stigma of their past.

But there is another identity, an interior one. To be a Nuba means to be strong, able to bear a thousand episodes of suffering and marginalization without losing one's identity, and proud to survive in such difficult circumstances. That man without hands, talking to D'Aybaury, told him his story, and all he had to say was, "I'm a Nuba." I have also heard the same declaration by people who recalled the most terrible moments of their lives. The innuendo was, "If I have managed to go through all that, it is because I am a Nuba. Had I not been one, I would have died, or given up a long time ago." They are fully conscious of their resilience, as when they practice their martial arts.

At the same time they are conscious of their diversity. There is no contradiction between saying "I am a Nuba" and seeing dwellings, in a village a few hours march away, built in a completely different style from those in his own. They too say "I am a Nuba" there. Not only the housing units are different, but also the traditions and the language. The expression "I am a Nuba" takes this plurality for granted.

Another characteristic trait is their keen sense of individuality blended with a living community spirit, and their capacity to reason together. Their tradition shows this: their chiefs are not autocratic, but acting in a democratic tradition founded on dialogue and palavering. The political organization is very much decentralised. There is an elder, or better a group of them respected by all, but no overall chief with powers of life and death as Comboni had supposed. In 1992, for instance, they decided to continue the war after a moment of deep crisis. The decision was taken in an assembly of all the Nuba groups of the zones controlled by the SPLM/A. That convention became an annual affair.

In religious affairs the same personal individuality prevails. Among the Dinka or the Shilluk the group prevails: when one becomes a Catholic it is because the family has opted for the Catholic faith. Among the Nuba they meet, they discuss, but everyone chooses independently. So it was in Kuwa's family. A younger brother reminisces:

> Yousif was a Muslim, like our parents and all of us, but he told me that no one ought to be discriminated against. In religion, he accepted things as they were, without fretting too much: 'These are things of God, and there is no difference whether you are a Christian or a Muslim. Everyone ought to be treated as a citizen and brother.' Naturally when they imposed the Sharía'h on us, we were all against it at once. He had four children from his first wife Fatuma; despite his, and Fatuma's, being Muslims, all the four children have become Christians. One actually, for some time, haboured the dream of joining the seminary...."

Rights-Hungry South Sudan

J went to southern Sudan for the first time in 1988, shortly after arriving in Nairobi from Zambia, where I had helped to launch the Comboni magazine *New People*.

In those years the SPLA regularly destroyed not only churches in the zones of southern Sudan it occupied, but also the parish archives, and took missionaries prisoners. The last two of them to remain in SPLA area were two Combonis, Frs Raphael Cefalo and Joseph Pellerino. In 1986 they were also taken prisoners and held for two months. There was no negotiating table between the SPLA and the Combonis. The first had their rearguard based in Nairobi, and the second dubbed them as Marxist-Leninists. I insisted that it was necessary to dialogue with them, and began to establish informal contacts.

That very year in Sudan there was a terrible famine, which caused 400 000 casualties, much more than the crisis of ten years later. But the international media said nothing about it, since the famine was ravaging the so-called "liberated" territories. The SPLA, furthermore, was too weak to manage a viable communication system. A member of the NGO Norwegian Aid, based in Khartoum, understood that the only way of relieving the situation was from the south, i.e. from Kenya. In July he contacted the Comboni Superior in Nairobi, who in turn contacted me.

The Norwegian asked me to accompany him by light aircraft to Kapoeta, the town nearest to the Kenya border, recently taken by the SPLA.

We took off from Lodwar, as the Lokichoggio facilities manned by OLS did not exist then. As we had Kapoeta in sight, the SPLA officer with us warned: "They tell me to land from the East, because westwards our anti-aircraft unit is at the ready." The pilot banked fast and we landed without problems.[8]

On disembarking we saw military men everywhere. We were received by Commander Edward Lino, a Dinka Catholic, still in the high ranks of the SPLA. I insisted on visiting the church. Embarrassed, he accompanied me to see the destruction: the disorder was total: vestments and books were on the ground everywhere. That was my first contact with southern Sudan.

The second contact was more complex. At the end of February 1989 the SPLA had occupied Torit after a siege of several months. They had captured Bishop Paride Taban, his priest John Baptist, both Sudanese, and two European missionaries: Fr Jean Lavacher, French, the last White Father left in the whole of Sudan, and Leo Traynor, Irish, of the St Patrick Missionary Society. In Nairobi a group of Church people of which I was part, was thinking of what to do, when an Irish layman, Enda Byrne, arrived from Khartoum with the aim of trying to get in touch with Bishop Taban, and with the support of some friends. Also, Fr Michael Schultheis SJ of the Jesuit Refugee Service and personal friend of Fr Arrupe their ex-General, had some money for such emergencies.

We organized a trip to Kapoeta to try and intervene in favour of the captives. The puny SPLA office in Nairobi gave us a visa and we left. We landed in Lodwar, received there by the Irish bishop who had promised us a car. We made it to Lokichoggio and there tried to contact the Turkana chief, a Catholic, whose name we had been given. "Loki" (as Lokichoggio is fondly known) was at the

---

[8]   Mike Grenell, the pilot, crashed a few weeks later in the Didinga Mountains. He was killed.

time a tiny village, which nevertheless had been bombed, scarcely a month before, by one of the Antonov aircraft that took off from Juba every now and then trying to hit some SPLA position or other. The pilots of the Russian aircraft were Libyans on loan to the Khartoum Government. They were not familiar with the zone, and furthermore they had to fly high to avoid flak. The Sudanese people have a poor opinion of Libyan pilots. Briefly, they bombed Loki mistaking it for Kapoeta, which lay some 120 kilometres north-west.

We found Martin, our contact. On asking him whether we could reach Kapoeta, he was very vague: "The road to Kapoeta… yes, provided it doesn't rain… but I can guarantee an escort only up to the border." We left early in the morning. Loki was already a quagmire. We braved a storm that promised nothing good, and reached Kapoeta in the evening. The only sign that we were there was finding two young sentries squatting by a fire.

The SPLA did not exactly welcome us. They gave us a room where to spend the night, under strict surveillance. Next morning an armed man came to wish us good morning. He said he was not a Christian, but had a good memory of a priest who had given him a pair of shoes many years back. The priest was Augustine Baroni, former Bishop of Khartoum, now deceased. I reflected, "How strange. One works for a lifetime to announce the Gospel and is remembered for a pair of shoes." About 7 am, another commander arrived, and somewhat haughtily said: "You have no permission to be here. Last night I could have ordered you shot. Now you are under house arrest until we ascertain that what you say is true." He returned in the afternoon:

"I do not acknowledge the person who issued you the visa given in Nairobi."

"How come? He is one of the SRRA, the humanitarian wing of the SPLA!"

"No matter, *I* do not acknowledge him."

One of the problems with the SPLA is that each one of them in his area considers himself to be pope and king. And he articulated:

"Garang (John Garang de Mabior, the then leader of the SPLA) is not contactable by radio. You are my prisoners. Do not go away from this house until the issue is clarified."

In reality we were able to wander around the place, but always under surveillance. I met an old teacher, who asked me to his "office" at the school. He showed me *Select stories from the Gospel* translated into Toposa by Fr Spagnolo in the 1940s. He was in Nairobi at the time. When I brought a copy to him, he wept with emotion.

I also saw the nutrition centre, seen during an early visit. Now it was clean and in order. About noon some thousand children queued for their rations. They were frighteningly thin, but not dramatically so. Some were shy, others, bolder, were quite ready to pose for a photo. On my return I wrote:

> They do not notice poverty, thinness, or their body full of sores. These are everyday occurrences. They have known nothing else: perhaps that ten-year old boy is in reality 14: his growth has been stunted by chronic malnutrition. He must have seen tragedies that I will not see in the whole of my life.

Our guardians were good, they treated us very well and we had no problem. No sooner our presence became known, than crowds of people came to see us. A young man, who introduced himself as a seminarian, whispered into my ear that the bishop was at Kodipo, and that everyone was alive. All knew it, except our mean commander, who feigned ignorance about the very existence of a bishop. It was obvious that our detention was his whim, and that he could have contacted Garang by radio any time he wanted. We insisted and were allowed to remain for a few days. We were able to visit a refugee (or prisoner) camp at Kor Machi, and to gather first hand information about humanitarian emergency help in the area. We were also able to have a serious meeting with some of the members of the civil administration. I dropped a hint: "How would you see the presence of missionaries here? I am authorized to speak on behalf of people who could be here in a matter of months, weeks perhaps." They replied,

We respect the missionaries. We have studied in their schools and know how much they have done for us. But we don't approve of their presence now. They would only exacerbate the clash between Christianity and Islam, thus distorting the true reasons for our struggle. For humanitarian work we have enough qualified personnel here on the ground.

Some reasons were convincing; others less so. Our interlocutors surprised us for being people with university education. But they were actually saying, "If you come to be missionaries in a strict sense, we are not interested; if you want to help us with human development, give us money and we shall make good use of it. There is no need for you to bother." In fact we appeared more of a busybody than the group of Americans who had landed at Kapoeta with a flight of the Catholic Relief Service (CRS) and taken off immediately after offloading their cargo. They had stayed a few hours, without leaving the house assigned to them.

We also visited the hospital and wrote to John Garang, who we were given to know, was about to come to Kapoeta. We intended to propose to him to have missionaries in the zones controlled by his Movement and to have reliable, fresh news about the captive bishop and his priests. We intended to celebrate Mass next day, Sunday 2nd April. As we looked for the commander to hand him the letter for Garang, he forestalled us. "I was looking for you. You have seen everything there was to be seen and now you had better return to Loki.

We tried to negotiate, trying to stay at least until Sunday Mass. He displayed a long list of reasons, one less credible than the other, especially about our security: "You must leave now, within an hour at most. Thus you will have left Sudan before evening."

We left under military escort. A few kilometres further on we crossed a UNICEF vehicle. Was security therefore only our problem?

Back in Nairobi, I drafted a report for the superior of my congregation. Shortly afterwards a Kenyan friend proposed to me "to meet a high ranking SPLA politician." He was speaking of Lam Akol, the then SPLA "Foreign Minister."

I met him for the first time in a Nairobi pizzeria. I was trying to talk to him about the bishop under arrest and of the situation. He attacked me with the usual Marxist-Lenninist rhetoric: the church that has done nothing, the Combonis who say they came to save Sudan but they only meant the North, opened schools only there and not in the South, etc.

I thought: if I rebut the charges energetically, it will be the end of our negotiations even before they have begun. But to keep silent I cannot. Finally I blurted out:

> I've heard such stories thousands of times: in Guinea-Bissau, and in Lusaka, from the South Africans of the ANC. But at least in the liberated zones of Guinea-Bissau, before independence, I saw the important basic political work done there by the PAIGC. They made the people aware... You don't do even that. All I have seen is weapons. If you wish I can show you the report I have drafted for my General Directors.

To my surprise, Akol did not react. He appeared puzzled. Then he asked for the report. A few days later he called me: "You are right, *Abuna,* I agree with you, we are weak in such things, the Movement does not function in raising people's awareness."

That's how my relations with Akol began. Today we are friends.

Some weeks later, as I was proceeding towards publishing the first issue of *New People,* in Nairobi, the Comboni superior came for a visit. I briefed him and suggested that he meet Akol so as to establish contacts with the SPLA and propose to them a Comboni presence in South Sudan. I added that the man was reasonable.

Fr Francis Pierli agreed, but said he would ask Fr Milani, one of the advisers, to do so on his behalf.

On Sunday 28th May three of us met in the offices of the journal. Milani asked Akol what the SPLA expected of the Combonis, and on what conditions it was ready to admit them in their territory.

> We would ask the Combonis to open schools, to make sure that aid actually got to the people, and scholarships for our young people to study in Kenya. See to it that our young people study and we shall leave you free to evangelise.

Analysing the situation, Lam Akol pointed out the progressive arabisation and Islamisation of the Sudan, a country that "once upon a time was Christian." The reference is to the ancient Nubian kingdoms. The Sudan government did not hide its intentions: it was replacing the British educational system in the schools of the South with the Arab one. Lam also defended the SPLA from the accusation of communism, which had alienated from it the favour of the United States "and of other European nations" now siding with Libya, Iran and Iraq with Khartoum. "It's a prejudice, based on the fact that the SPLA has leaned on Ethiopia." Ethiopia in those days was headed by the "Red Negus" Mengistu Haile Mariam.

As arranged beforehand with Fr Milani, before concluding the agreement I broached the subject:

"But you know what experience I have had with the SPLA and its commanders…"

Lam paused, and after some silent moments, he said:

"*Abuna*, Msgr Paride has been released. I saw him during Easter. He expressed the desire for the Church to work in the liberated zones. Go to Torit and see him and his missionaries free. They are free to come to Nairobi if they wish. I give you my word."

I took off with the first flight of the Lutheran World Federation, with a cargo of food and under the aegis of the United Nations. The aircraft had to land in a corkscrew dive to avoid government antiaircraft fire placed all round the town. On the 7th June I found the four. They looked rather ill after 90 days "in protection," even though they tried to dissimulate serenity. We asked to celebrate Mass. As we vested, Taban whispered:

"They humiliated us! They ill-treated us!"

He refused, as did the Sudanese priest, to come to Nairobi. Before we left he said:

"This is my country and this is my people. I am here with open arms. If the government were truly on the side of the people, this continuous war would have no reason to be. But perhaps for the first time the international community has begun to take notice of

Sudan. There's a lot of talk about South Africa, and rightly so. But what is the difference between here and there? Information. And yet, the amount of injustice that the people of southern Sudan have had to bear is perhaps worse than what's happening in South Africa. And the world takes no notice! I still remember when the elders of my village told me stories of the northern slave raids. We are still living those times. There's no improvement, there's no consideration of the human dignity of the southern people. I want my bones to rest at Torit. I will leave Torit when there is real peace in Sudan."

Whys and Wherefores
of a 20 Year War

J t is now time to probe the reasons for this war. The starting point is the enormous historical differences within a country of 2.5 million square kilometres with some 30 million people. The obvious dividing line between North and South is the parallel of latitude 10° N, along which lies an uninhabited zone.

Geographically, the North is arid, except for the Nile; the South is rich in vegetation and water courses. Ethnically the North is largely of distant Arab origin (except the Nuba and the two million refugees from the South that crowd the environs of Khartoum); the South is peopled by some 652 "tribes" (in the colonial sense) but in a constant state of flux and mix. A Dinka friend of mine said to me "It is not an exaggeration to say that not one person in southern Sudan lives today where he lived 20 years ago."

The biggest ethnic groups are the Dinka, the Shilluk and the Nuer. It has already been remarked how the Crown, aware of Sudanese complexity, had adopted the system of *indirect rule* and of "closed districts" common to its colonies on the whole continent. It was also thinking whether to associate the South to neighbouring territories under its rule rather than to the North. The Shilluk, for instance, are related to the Kenya Luo and the Uganda Acholi. Richard Gray, who taught history at the University of Khartoum for 30 years, described the progress to independence as follows:

> Only about 1930 did the British reach an agreement with the southern people, while learning how to govern according to their customs and traditions. For a single generation there was peace in the South, but to maintain it, it was necessary to isolate it from all Northern influence, including Islam, and to keep it underdeveloped. Economic development was concentrated in the North, with cotton plantations in the region of Gezira, the fertile "island" between the White and Blue Nile. The British counted on time to develop the area, so that the first secondary school opened there only in 1948. During the Anglo-Egyptian negotiations after the war' the US, fearful of Soviet influence in Egypt, pushed for an early solution. When the British administrators left the South in 1955, the territory was attached to the North. The operation was seen as passing from one form of colony to another. The civil war thus began. The British bear the greatest responsibility, even though never acknowledged.[9]

The enormous difference in economic development between North and South was very obvious before independence, even though masked by the British administration umbrella. One could see what intractable problems would arise in the future.

Independence, promulgated on 1st January 1956, consecrated the present boundaries when war was already in the air. There had been a revolt in Torit in August 1955. The short-lived period of calm did not favour a smooth handing over. The southern MPs voted for independence, naively trusting in a resolution by the northern MPs according to which the latter had undertaken to take "in full consideration" the wishes of the South for a federal State. The Torit rebels recruited forces and launched the secessionist movement called *Anya-nya*.[10] Israel gave them military assistance after the Six-Day War in the Middle East. Because of the war, in 1964 the Khartoum government expelled the entire missionary personnel from the South: 214 Catholics and 28 Protestants. They

---

[9] Richard Gray, "La storia e il Nilo," in *Sudan, un popolo senza diritti – Atti del Forum.* 17-18 settembre 1999, Campagna Italiana per la pace e il rispetto dei diritti umani in Sudan, Milano 2000, pp. 7-8. Our translation.

[10] In the Madi language, viper venom.

53

were accused of actively supporting the guerrillas. After the 1958 coup the country was under military rule. Colonel Nimeiry's 1969 coup made possible the Addis Ababa Agreement of 1972, in which Colonel Joseph Lagu was a signatory for the Anyanya. Nimeiry was not really convinced of southern claims, but at least he had understood that a military solution was impossible, and that a better option was to make Sudan governable. The Addis Ababa Agreement had granted the South a large amount of self-government, which included a local Parliament. Prof. Gray goes on:

> Three questions arose during this period. The first was desertification in the South, particularly felt by the Nuba, threatened as they were by mechanized agriculture financed by rich Arabs; the second was the automatic weapons in the hands of the Baggara, who started using them against the Nuba and the Nile pastoralists; the third was the Jonglei Canal, designed to increase the flow of the Nile to the advantage of the North and of Egypt, but feared by the South, which felt little protected. And finally there was the discovery of oil in both North and South, which caused the breaking off of the Agreement. War broke out once more with the advent of the SPLA headed by John Garang, who did not aim at secession as much as to play a part in the politics of the New Sudan.

The SPLA was founded on May 16th 1983, when the Bor garrison, with its commander Kerubino Kwanyin Bol, refused to be moved to the North. Khartoum sent lieutenant colonel John Garang to quell the mutiny. The officer, a Dinka, asked nothing better than to head the 500 rebels himself.

The political climate was changing: Nimeiry was no longer the man he was in 1972. He needed to reacquire the consensus of the North and therefore tried to ingratiate Hassan el-Turabi, a charismatic Islamic fundamentalist leader. In September of that same year 1983 Nimeiry promulgated the *Sharia'h*, the law of Islam, thus adding fuel to the fire.

In its first political manifesto, the SPLA declared not to want secession, but "to struggle to found a unitary socialist Sudan." Hostilities coutinued until the ceasefire agreement of May 26, 2004: The war finally ended on January 9 2005 with the signing of the

Comprehensive Peace Agreement (CPA) in Nairobi. Tragically, at the same time, a new front was opening in the Darfur.

Nimeiry was overthrown in April 1985 while in the US, which had always supported him. The next regime was more open to southern requests, but Garang, making use of familiar tactics, dictated conditions unacceptable by Khartoum. In a year General Swar el-Dahab turned the country into a parliamentary democracy. The elected PM was Sadiq el-Mahdi, a descendant of the Mahdi. He was intent on crafting a solution for the southern question, and tried to resist religious pressure towards total and rapid Islamization. It was his undoing. An umpteenth coup, three years later, just on the eve of an accord with the SPLA, brought to power the Islamic National Front, representing the most intransigent Islamic faction. Another general ascended the throne in July 1989: Omar Hassan el-Bashir, who is still in power. During the first ten years of tenure he had an *éminence grise* called Turabi, theologian of the Islamic Brethren politically represented by the Islamic National Front. Towards the end of 1999 Bashir ousted Turabi from the levers of power and placed him under house arrest. Such exercise of raw power was no doubt influenced by the opening of the oil wells in Bentiu, Upper Nile region.

An oil pipeline takes the crude to Port Sudan on the Red Sea, bringing in one million dollars a day, as much as the cost of OLS. Making use of the stick with Turabi and of the carrot with the oil, Bashir consolidated power. He mollified the European Union abroad, and on the domestic scene he gave himself a veneer of democracy by dialoguing with both Sadiq el-Mahdi, whom he himself had overthrown, and Nimeiry. Both came back from their exile of many years together with many people at the opposition. Taking distances from Turabi proved farsighted: after September 11 Bashir could afford to condemn terrorism, adding that he had given information to the American secret service about the staying of Osama bin Laden in Sudan. Osama and Turabi were close friends.

Among the actors of the Sudanese drama there is also the National Democratic Alliance, which unites a number of opposition groups. IGAD, the Inter-Government Authority on Development, is the regional economic organization and includes Sudan, Eritrea, Ethiopia, Djibouti, Kenya, Somalia and Uganda.

The war ought to be seen in this wide context, not simplified as a racial or religious conflict between an Arab, Islamized North and a Christian, and African traditional religious-oriented South. The confusion is been fostered by the media. The war has been provoked by a systematic violation of human rights having its origin in history, culture (and therefore religion), and which gets tangled with economic and geopolitical international motivations. The oilfields in fact are mostly in the South. They are to be found in an immense territory also endowed with agricultural and pastoralist resources: millions of heads of cattle are raised in the lands of the Shilluk, Dinka and Nuer. The opposition to the Jonglei Canal, stopped on the eve of its completion, is due to two reasons: it cuts into two the Dinka cattle-raising area, so that the drained lands of the Sudd,[11] the largest wetland on earth, would immediately be colonized by agribusiness people from the North.

The second Forum of the Sudan Campaign had as a theme "Water and Oil: war and human rights." The two headings of the Naivasha Agreement of September 2003 had to do with division of power and the distribution of wealth, first of all the oil income. There were also questions like the "marginal" zones of Abyei, the southern Blue Nile and the Nuba Mountains. The religious and cultural factor acts as a sort of catalyser, introduced by those with a vested interest in fomenting "holy wars" and other forms of fanaticism. The fundamental questions are those of economic and social justice, the dignity of one third of the population of the country, and the right to self-determination within a federal State. In the 1970s Yousif used to say to Abdelaziz:

---

[11]   The word is Arabic for "hindrance, obstacle." The canal was to be 360 km long, from Malakal to Bor.

"The problem is not circumscribed to the Nuba. The problem of underdevelopment involves the whole of Sudan, both in the South and in the East. Take the Beja: they suffer and live in worse conditions than we do here on the Nuba Mountains. And what about the Darfur, the land you come from? Don't you have the same problems? Let us therefore struggle for the liberation of the entire Sudan, not only of the Nuba Mountains!"

Abdelaziz rebutted:

"But it is too big a problem..."

"True. But if you want change on the Nuba Mountains, the entire Sudan must change."

The Children's Red Army

My entry into Sudan was by now sanctioned. After meeting Akol, my superiors had entrusted me with "maintaining the necessary contacts" with the SPLA. In September 1989 I was on the move once again in the company of the first Comboni returning to SPLA-controlled South Sudan to stay there. He was José Oscar Flores López, a Mexican, going to work with Bishop Taban.

Later I travelled with other confreres, who like Flores, went to establish themselves in the old mission sites. A longer trip was that with Fr Milani. We reached Kapoeta by car, proceeded to Torit on the Didinga Mountains, finally to Loa and to where the Nile enters Sudan from Uganda. In Loa we met Fr Mario Riva, who had just escaped death in a rather startling fashion. The previous week government aircraft had bombed the place, obviously trying to hit the mission. They missed it, although some bombs fell uncomfortably close. A few days later, on a Sunday, Fr Mario had just pulled the rope to ring the bell, a rather big one, when someone urgently called him. That saved his life. The belfry, cracked by the bombs, collapsed at the first peal of the great bronze bell, which fell just where he had been seconds before.

The most important event of that trip, however, was meeting the vanguard of the *Red Army* about to arrive in Kapoeta. They were thousands of young boys! The story is still murky. The SPLA version is that many thousands of orphan boys and girls marched towards Ethiopia during the 1988 famine, but the girls, weaker, were left behind or died. At Fugnido, an Ethiopian village of the Gambela region, next to the Sudanese border, the UN High Commissioner for Refugees (UNHCR) had set up a camp for 35-50 000 children. When Mengistu fell, in May 1991, his last defenders were the men of the SPLA, who saw in him a safe ally. The SPLA quickly abandoned its Ethiopian rear positions, fearing the reaction of the new government. Its leaders left for Nairobi by car or as best they could, urging all southern Sudanese to leave Ethiopia. The Fugnido children panicked, and re-entered Sudan. The border is an escarpment, which in five kilometres drops from 1 000 metres of altitude to the Nile marshlands. The rainy season was particularly heavy. They died in their hundreds trying to cross the water courses; the rest found themselves trapped in a completely uninhabited, inhospitable country. In a matter of weeks they exhausted the few provisions they had taken with them, after which they tried fishing in the river and in the marshes. But even this was very dangerous. And on top of that the Khartoum government bombed them.

On becoming aware of the situation, we went to the UNHCR representative with Maryknoll priest Carroll Houle.

"Can't you do anything?"

"They are not refugees; they are now in their own country. There's nothing we can do."

Then we went to the Red Cross:

"We are in a position to intervene only when both belligerents call us."

Nobody seemed willing to get involved. Operation Lifeline Sudan mumbled:

"We don't know the situation well... We are *super partes*... without Government authorisation we cannot intervene..."

All hands were tied.

I grabbed some money left over from what Fr Milani had given me during the great famine, chartered a flight and undertook a mad journey. Alone with the pilot (an American I never saw again) in the small Caravan aircraft, I was carrying a tonne of tinned meat. I knew it would not solve anything, but it was a sort of first aid, and once there I could shoot a video to publicise the children's plight.

We left Nairobi at the crack of dawn, fuelled at Lodwar and made a technical landing at Lokichoggio. Half an hour from the Pochala airstrip we hit a storm, which mercilessly tossed the aircraft like a feather. I really thought it was the end. Until the pilot told me he could not afford to land in thick mud: had he dared, he would have got stuck there for days on end.

"I'm sorry Father, I can't land. I'm going back."

Even if one has paid, the last choice is not in one's hands. And it was not all. When the sky cleared, he said:

"To tell you the truth, I'm lost. Can you help?"

We were flying by dead reckoning, because the aircraft had no GPS system. Further, you never knew which villages were SPLA and which Government. I ventured:

"I know Kapoeta. There is a river next to it, and we are flying southwards...we are bound to overfly it."

A quarter of an hour later I saw a rivulet. Luckily I had seen Kapoeta from the air four or five times before. We landed and refuelled. It must have been 1:30 p.m., too late to retry. On the Equator darkness falls very swiftly. Crestfallen, we opted for Nairobi. And as if it that had not been enough, we hit another storm over Naivasha. Hailstones of unusual size were machine-gunning the aircraft, but the pilot was unruffled. I ate the last crust of bread. I got home exhausted. The nervous tension that day was terrific.

Next day I was back at the Red Cross. They had got wind of my attempt, and decided to spring into action.

Meanwhile the children had regrouped and stopped, waiting for the ground to dry up. Fr Benjamin, a Sudanese priest from the Diocese of Rumbek, had joined them. He had great ascendancy over those boys between the ages of seven and 16. When the column resumed the march, the Red Cross followed them with food airdrops. They marched 600 kilometres to Kapoeta.

They stopped there for a long time, and it was there that John Garang christened them the *Jiec Amar, Red Army*. Later, independent organisations like Human Rights Watch issued hard-hitting reports in respect of the SPLA, accusing them of recruiting an army of children soldiers. Among them, according to Peter Adwok Nyaba, a high-ranking SPLA officer but opposing Garang, were 3 000 Nuba children forcibly abducted from their families and let to die of hunger in the military training camp of Bilpam, in Ethiopia. In September 2000 a UN special correspondent for human rights reported that the forced recruitment of children in the South had not ceased.

When Garang smelled the wind of change after the collapse of the Berlin Wall, the sobriquet *Red Army* was no longer politically correct. The children left their weapons at Kapoeta and reached Lokichoggio as refugees in May-June 1992. The UNHCR set up a camp for them at Kakuma, south of Loki. I went there with an Italian journalist and a Kenyan on the staff of *New People*. We arrived as the rear of the children's column was still crossing the border. I celebrated the Eucharist there and then with Fr Benjamin.

Late in the afternoon, as we were about to go back, I heard high shouting behind me. Daniel, the Italian, was somersaulting, with a following of hundreds of children lost in admiration. The general joy was sky-high.

The Liberation
Movement Spilts

J n 1989 three US missionaries – Frs Caroll Houle, MM, Mike Schultheis, SJ, and Sr Fredericka Jacob – a Kenyan journalist, Joseph Ngala and I had founded People for Peace in Africa (PPA) in Nairobi. The initial aim was to stimulate the Nairobi religious environment into action towards peace. Kenya, besides its domestic problems, is affected by the wars and struggles of Central and East Africa. It is in fact not only the organisational centre of many international agencies and diplomatic representations, but also the target of many refugees in search of opportunities for a good life.

No sooner I arrived in Nairobi than I realized how important a commitment to peace was. Faced with the many brands of conflict, I was very much aware of the lack of preparation, mine as much as that of those interested in such problems. When we launched PPA, we immediately realised that in reality none of us priests, sisters and the scanty lay people involved had adequate instruments, or even formation, to intervene in a conflict, either to promote peace or to keep it. And yet this is one of the Church's fundamental tasks today, which cannot be set aside. On the occasion of the 1994 African Synod there had been the proposal to include in the sacrament of reconciliation a rite for reconciling groups until then in conflict with one another, considering the fact that such communal rites already exist in Africa.

We got involved in an awkward internal affair regarding the SPLA. On Thursday 16th May 1991 there were great celebrations, as it was the eighth anniversary of the start of the war. In Kapoeta I had taken shots from the vehicle with my video camera. In the evening a security man came to see me: "Give me the camera and the videocassettes. You had no authority to film." After protesting, I did as told, but managed to hand him blank cassettes. Then I went to the commander to remonstrate. He was Pagan Amoun, who in 2003 would lead the SPLA delegation to Khartoum. Then something incredible happened. Two days later Amoun gave me back the cassettes, with profuse apologies ("I didn't know, they acted behind my back"). He had contacted Akol by radio. Towards the end of August I received a letter: "*Abuna*, I have always been in good terms with you, we see eye to eye in most issues... I am about to undertake a dangerous mission. You have never met my wife, I entrust her to you. She will soon be in Nairobi and will get in touch with you." It was three o'clock in the afternoon, in the *New People's* office. At 5pm. the BBC reported that Riek Machar Teny-Dhurgon, Lam Akol Ajawin and the lesser known Gordon Kong Chuol had overthrown Garang. They issued the *Nasir Declaration* dated 28th August 1991:

> During the past eight years John Garang has headed the Movement in the most dictatorial and autocratic fashion... To save the Movement from an imminent collapse, it has been decided to relieve him of his leadership of the SPLM/A.

The Declaration emphasised "militarism" and the "violation of human rights" that had held sway in the Movement up to then. Lam had, in his letter, given me his wife's telephone number. I called Rebecca Joshua Ohwaci: she was unaware of anything, although she was the bearer of the Nasir letter from eastern Upper Nile.

That's how the SPLA split. The overtrowing of Garang was only on paper. In fact, most of the SPLA remained with him. According to Lam, the primary reason for the spilt was that the Central Committee of the Movement was never convened, not even when important decisions were to be taken. When finally Garang convoked them all to Torit at the beginning of September 1991, the dissidents found out that it was a trap: they risked prison or death, since Garang was aware of what they were up to. Instead of clashing in the open, "Alpha Beta," "Sennar" and "Ivory" decided to present Garang with a declaration of *fait accompli.*

On the first page of the *Nasir Declaration,* Lam's still unpublished manuscript, Lam recalls that on the 17th June, at the end of a crucial meeting, Machar announced his imminent wedding two hours later. After the festivities Lam, on going to bed, asked himself whether Machar had not in fact underestimated the impact of the political gesture they were about to undertake, and the hard challenges waiting for them. Furthermore, the wife was a *khawaja,* a white woman. Her name was Emma McCune, British, a fascinating and rather vivacious girl working for a humanitarian organisation. Her behaviour had raised a few hackles. Someone wrote that she "dreamt marrying the first president of southern Sudan" a Nuer who had already a wife and three children. She is portrayed in a movie called *Emma's War.*

At PPA we were challenged by that split. We wrote two letters, one to each of the parties, manifesting our disappointment and declaring our availability to help them overcome the crisis if they wanted to. Akol answered first, agreeing. Garang dragged his feet, but also agreed. The peace talks began in October, dragged on to Christmas and re-started in February, but only for a few days. The initiative was backed by Ambassador Bethuel Kiplagat, the then Permanent Secretary in the Kenyan Foreign Ministry and Garang's good friend. He is a unique personage. As a Protestant pastor, he had founded the National Council of Churches of Kenya (NCCK) back in the 1960s. He was then invited to Khartoum to repeat the experience. Thence he was sent to Geneva, and recalled by President Moi. After a period of formation in Israel, he served in the Ministry for almost a decade. Since the end of his mandate he has kept some political weight even beyond the Moi era. In 2003 he was appointed as negotiator of the Somali National Reconciliation Conference.

Through him, who also took part in some of the talks, substantial help came from Kenyan diplomacy. They furnished vehicles for the bodyguards of the two delegations, and paid for their boarding and lodging in Nairobi, where the talks were held in a spirituality centre at Langata. The results were nil. Officially, the head of the Nasir faction was Machar, but Akol headed the delegation. He had always overseen its foreign relations. And he outclassed everyone: at the end of each day the so-called "Torit" faction had been cajoled into agreeing with him. Politically they had been ruined. Garang, intelligently, did not come to the talks. The leader of his delegation was James Wani Igga, a Zande. His instructions came from Garang, whom he telephoned for every issue. The reply was invariably "no." The delegates had no choice but to agree.

The only thing they agreed to was the release of some 40 political prisoners in Garang's hands, except four: Kerubino, a rather astute, egocentric personage, the rebellious commander of the Bor garrison. Arok Thon Arok, ex-colonel of the government army and in charge of the secret services on passing to the SPLA, John Kulang Puot and Martin Makour Aleyou. The first three were members of the High Command. Garang categorically opposed their liberation. They would remain in detention at Torit, where the head of the prisons was an authentic murderer. We agreed that Fr Houle and I would travel to Torit to receive the prisoners from Wani Igga's hands. But the thing dragged for a long time, which is understandable: the prisoners had been maltreated, and needed some time to be presentable again. In January we got to Torit and interviewed them one by one under a tree. They told us hair-raising stories: some were half blind, forced to dig the prison, in the shape of a well with tunnels, with their own hands. They ate whenever the sentries remembered to throw them some food from the top. Some had not seen sunlight for two or three years. I have since preserved video recordings of those interviews.

When we mentioned summoning an aircraft to take them away, Igga hedged and started cooking up excuses: "It's not possible... we have to wait..." Carroll told me that he was ready to stay on, while I would have to travel to Nairobi to look after *New People* and talk to Garang. Quite honestly, Garang said that he was not moved enough to liberate "his worst enemies." With these words he quashed what remained of the negotiations, which as far as he was concerned had been irrelevant. "I'm the one who takes decisions here," he said.

Defeated, I sent word to Carroll to come to Nairobi, as there was nothing doing. Some months later some prisoners were indeed released, after restoring their physical conditions somewhat and indoctrinating them not to speak too much. The more dangerous, like Kerubino, Arok Thon and Atem Gualdit managed to escape, simply by convincing their guards of the goodness of their cause. They went to Uganda, where I visited them. In August-September 1992 they came to Nairobi as Lam Akol's guests.

The Nasir faction was at its golden moment. Prestigious political exiles joined the group. They had no military power, but enjoyed a great prestige among the Sudanese. The important ones were "uncle" Joseph Oduho, about 60-65, and Clement Mboro, a pure politician. Oduho supported the Anya-nya from the beginning, and particularly Fr Saturnino Lohure, assassinated in 1967. Oduho had always enjoyed a reputation for impartiality, mostly due to his being a Lotuko, therefore not involved with any of the big ethnic groups, but known for its determination. Oduho had taken part in the 1972 Addis talks, where he obtained important concessions, which extended his leadership from the Lotuko to the whole South.

Oduho had tasted Garang's prisons. Once released, as the consummate politician he was, he did not seek vengeance but continued with his impartial stance. Lam was right in trying to co-opt him into the leadership of the new movement. Whenever I met "uncle" in meetings that they held in the offices of *New People*, I always noticed his invariable mediatory role, even when an initiative sprang from a net opposition to Garang. Oduho always wanted to leave a door open to a possible reunification, albeit on precise conditions. Catastrophe struck when Riek Machar reacted to the trap of Kongor by unleashing the Nuer against the Dinka. In a matter of months the SPLA of Nasir lost the support of the International Community and of OLS, which on paper was not supposed to occupy itself with politics but on the ground it threw its weight around quite considerably. It was enough to be accepted or not by the OLS as a representative of a given population of a given territory to receive, or lose, a substantial authority and economic aid. Lam Akol knew it well, on trying to get recognition for his small group SPLA-United, which controlled only the Shilluk. That is why Dr Meo's CCM and another Swiss NGO were able to operate in that area without OLS support. Furthermore, OLS was not authorised to transport military personnel, but it is well known that Garang's officers had flown in its aircraft. So that when OLS said "sorry, we have no seat for either Akol or Machar," it was clear in whose favour the scales were tipped.

One evening, at the end of an umpteenth meeting, Lam, Kerubino and Oduho – who was representing Commander Nyuon Bany,[12] decided to unite into a group called SPLM/A-United, to emphasise unity among the three groups by maintaining the original name of the Movement. Prof Barri Wanji, a Bari from the South, was also present. They intended to formalise the union in Sudan on a question of principle, albeit without Garang. They left for Kongor, and invited me to go with them. I was tempted, but I had also kept in touch with Garang's faction. As *People for Peace* we had to maintain distances. I could not make act of presence at a meeting that was clearly against Garang who at that moment looked like being a loser. I decided not to go, sparing myself trouble.

They left and the talks began, but Garang had let them into a trap. Panyagor, the site chosen for the meeting, had been entirely surrounded, including the airstrip. The attack was sudden, even though the security services had alerted them on the 27th morning. Lam Akol had noticed the reigning indiscipline of Riek Machar's

---

12 Bany was killed in a exchange of fire between the two factions.

men, and when under fire he had also verified the bad organisation of the chain of command. *Uncle* Oduho was taken prisoner and killed in cold blood, most certainly on Garang's orders by radio, as had happened in other cases. Lam, Thon and others succeeded in escaping. Riek's wife, Emma, arrived in Nairobi completely worn-out, to die some months later in a stupid car accident. She was not yet 30, and pregnant.

It was the beginning of the end for the SPLA-United, which survived only around Lam Akol. Riek had founded the SSIM (South Sudan Independence Movement), but by 1995 he was on his own. The rot set in. All the factions lost strength, also because the Americans had meanwhile forced their way in with their dollars, and bet on Garang as their favourite horse.

At the beginning of 1997 Lam Akol was fast losing ground. He came to Nairobi from Shilluk land, after my attempt to visit Kau-Nyaro. He was demoralised. Time passed and his troops were losing ground. All through August of that year he sent fax upon fax to Addis Ababa from Kibera, the Nairobi slum where he resided. He was petitioning Addis for military and other aid as granted to him in the past. Addis did not answer. The Americans had ordered Ethiopia not to support him anymore. Lam blurted out: "What am I to do? My men on the ground want ammunition and weapons. Should I play the hero and tell them to fight to the death? It would be very easy from here... I'll try to get as much political advantage as I can, given the situation." He declared a ceasefire, then went to meet a government delegation and signed a declaration of intent, making the government believe that he was controlling a territory that in reality he wasn't. On September 20th, at Fashoda, the government signed an agreement with Lam, similar to the one signed earlier with Machar, where it was agreed that a referendum would be held within six years. It was the same transition period also foreseen in the agreement signed between the SPLA and the Khartoum government in May 2004.

After Fashoda, Lam was nominated Minister for Transport at Khartoum, where he remained in office for five years. At the same time he maintained control over his territory, the right to have his own army, and the right to become once again a beneficiary of OLS.

The six years of the agreement expired in March 2003. The government's inattention made him return to the SPLA in October. He had observed "changes in favour of democracy and the adoption of the principle of self-determination."

Another blow to Garang's opposition was an air crash in 1998 caused by human error, but which the SPLA-Mainstream tried to get credit for. A large group of faction representatives was touring the South to make sure that Kerubino's about-face did not jeopardise the existing agreements that held SPLA-United together.[13] At Nasir the plane missed the airstrip and crashed into the river Sobat. About 30 people died, including Thon Arok and the Sudan Vice President al-Zubair Mohammed Salih. Lam suffered only scratches. Arok Thon's loss was particularly serious, as he had a photographic memory of the events.

[13] Kerubino died in a 1999 fire exchange. He had endlessly commuted between the dissidents, the Movement and the government.

At Leer with the Nuer

L am Akol was instrumental in my meeting Yousif Kuwa. They had met in 1980, when Lam, back from his London degree in chemical engineering, had started teaching at the University of Khartoum. Yousif, 35 at the time, had just got his degree in economics from that same university. Lam's brother John had been Kuwa's classmate. Abdelaziz was another contemporary. He reminisces:

> Yousif had a lot of experience. He had become a teacher after finishing secondary school, so as to support his family. He was the first to earn a salary. He was courageous and daring. He was not happy with letting things be. He wanted to study so as to change things.

The decisive meeting took place at Philip Abbas Ghabboush's, a Nuba Anglican pastor, later founder and high prelate of an independent church. Shortly afterwards Ghabboush was arrested under the charge of having hatched a "racist plot" and prepared a coup. Later he was amnestied by Nimeiry. Before his going into hiding, Lam Akol was invited to witness a blood covenant between Ghabboush, Kuwa and Abdelaziz on an "unforgettable afternoon." Up to then Kuwa had entered politics as a representative in the regional Parliament, but he told Lam of his decision to join the SPLA. Two years later they met in a Cuban training camp together with Wani Igga.

Ghabboush, perhaps 80-plus today, is a picturesque, fighting type, a sort of grand patriarch of the Nuba. He was present at the

December 2002 General Nuba Conference under the mango trees at Kauda. An excellent speaker, he got a standing ovation after another when claiming "Kuwa and Abdelaziz are my sons!"

35 people, among them Kuwa and Abdelaziz, had founded the Komolo group in Khartoum in 1975. In Miri, Yousif's language, "komolo" means "youth." The name was not chosen at random, but to sidestep Ghabboush. Says Abdelaziz, "Komolo had been set up in opposition to the old Nuba political class. We wanted change. Ghabboush was not there, for we had not told him of our decision to join the SPLM/A. He got the news at the last moment, when Yousif decided to go public and asked me to go together to Ghabboush's house. He was taken aback, but reacted by giving us his blessing. 'It's the right thing to do. There is no alternative. I was looking for a young, daring man like you, capable of leading the flock and the Nuba into battle. I have been treated like a rag, and don't want the same thing to happen to you.' And thus, Ghabboush, founder of the Nuba General Union, in 1964, was one of the first to encourage us."

In 1993 the new Generalate of the Comboni relieved me from the task of keeping contacts with the SPLA in the name of the Institute. But before entering the Nuba world, I had another occasion to travel in South Sudan. I had met Martin Manyiel Ayuel, a most respected Dinka commander. He inspired trust, like Kuwa and Lam. His enormous prestige rested on his having convinced the entire garrison of Kajo-Kaji, near Nimule on the Uganda border, to defect en masse to the SPLA. He had thus captured a most important military position without firing a shot. He was a member of the Central Committee, very much loved and popular. At Kapoeta, another city where he acted as a commander, many of the Toposa boys born while he was in charge, are called Martin. It is an indisputable sign of his reputation.

Later he fell sick, probably of AIDS. The SPLA had no funds to treat him. I saw him for the last time, dying in a Nairobi hospital. My eyes began to open when I heard him whisper, in the presence of a very important Garang aide, "Garang is becoming the greatest obstacle to peace in the Sudan." In those years it was the only criticism of Garang aired openly. When the Movement split, Martin felt it deeply. He was the only one able to keep in touch with both factions. He told me: "Lam Akol and Riek Machar are not traitors. They are patriots. They don't see eye to eye with Garang, but this should not be a problem."

In October 1993 I travelled to Leer, as Kuwa had referred to when we first met. I was invited by Joseph Phal Mut, an exceptional Christian sent to me, as I would learn later, by Kerubino. Joseph had travelled to Nairobi with the express purpose of scouting the missionary centres for a priest to be sent to the Upper Nile region. He said that thousands of Catholics there were asking for a priest to administer the Sacraments. At the beginning no one took him seriously. There had never been a Catholic mission at Leer, a marshy Nuer area. It was known that the percentage of Nuer Catholics was very low, as the few Christians were mostly Presbyterians. The last official statistics for the Diocese of Malakal, of which Nuer country is part of, gave a figure of 37 100 Catholics for a population of 2.7 million people scattered over an area of 238 000 square kilometres. The civil war had restricted the movement of the bishop and a few of his priests to a small area around Malakal. When Phal Mut opened his notebooks with thousands of names of baptised people, no one believed him. But he, who had discovered the Christian faith while in the Fugnido refugee camp, in Ethiopia, did not give up.

One August day I was in the *New People* office when a visitor called. I saw a tall man with a particularly likeable countenance. "Could you please send a priest to Leer?" He showed his list of baptised to me and my confrere Paul Donohue. There were roughly 100 000 names, with dates, places and names of godparents. We decided to risk and go. We wanted to see personally what was going on. We spent a week in Leer, witnessing the incredible work of a fistful of young catechists under Phal Mut's leadership. We visited dozens of chapels built under clumps of savannah trees, and used as prayer centres for the inhabitants of the zone. We spoke to them. They knew the essentials of the Faith. We celebrated the Eucharist everywhere after administering the Sacrament of Reconciliation. Thousands of adult Christians had never seen a priest before.

In the absence of ecclesiastical structures, in a total state of deprivation, and in the middle of a harsh war, a whole people were coming to Christ, to the Church. The area had spurned all missionary efforts for a good century: the Comboni had arrived in 1904, but had succeeded in converting a handful of Shilluk. Now, the work of a semiliterate young man was bearing unsuspecting, overabundant fruit. There was no trace of Christians as late as 1982, when Fr Elvio Cellana, a missionary residing in Tonga, some 80km from Leer, had passed through with his motorbicycle during the dry season.

They called the catechists *Abuna* (Father). We also got the impression that they were celebrating some sort of Communion rite. Their faith and love for Jesus were serious and beyond dispute. They were also concerned about keeping their community in touch with the Church.

How could a man like Joseph Phal Mut achieve all that, in an area ranging from Leer all the way to Ethiopia? "With these," he would answer while hitting his legs with his hands. "They are the only thing the Lord has given me. Walking is the only thing I know how to do. Wherever I arrive, I teach what I know about Christ and the Church." In every place he formed young catechists, who continued his work after he left. The work increased and multiplied. I insisted:

"And how comes you didn't found your own church, as many others have?"

He hesitated, then replied:

"Can you announce darkness, after having seen the light? How could I preach myself, after knowing Jesus?"

That experience foretold the type of church I was going to find on the Nuba Mountains. Vincent Mojwok Nyeker, Bishop of Malakal, established a missionary presence in Leer following our visit, but the war erased it once again. Joseph was sent to study theology in Nairobi, but one evening he was struck by a lorry and killed.

After my visiting the Nuba Mountains, Bishop Mojwok, favourably impressed by our "raid" in the territory of his diocese, urged me not to forget the Shilluk. In May 1992 I had been in Tonga with Dr Meo, trying to convince him to open a dispensary. I returned there with Meo and Akol when news filtered about the split between the latter and Riek Machar. We had also tried to reach the place from the south, but had to abort the attempt. D'Aybaury didn't give up: he conceived the mad stunt of overflying the place with a powered micro-light, and take photos from the air, but the friend with the micro light died while circling Kilimanjaro.

Tonga means "end," the southernmost point of Shilluk land. I returned there in August 1995 immediately after visiting the Nuba Mountains. An official welcome committee was waiting for me at the airstrip. The walk from there to the old mission was memorable. I had taken less than an hour during my previous trip: now it took more than two. The rains had transformed the area into a quagmire. Less than 100 metres from the airstrip we were walking in a dense, slippery mud up to our ankles. Every step required a balancing act. Things improved on taking off my shoes and rolling up my trousers, but only for the first ten minutes. The mud became waist-high. Drummers and singers were unruffled. They did not slacken their effort a whit. Behind them we walked on paths baked by the hot sun, and which alternated with long watery, muddy stretches up to the grounds of the old mission.

The Shilluk are a world apart, from the Nuba as much as from the Dinka. The latter go to the river occasionally, to water their cattle, but generally speaking live away from water. The Shilluk, however "related" to the Dinka, live on the river, where they have developed a lifestyle of their own. In a sense they are even more isolated than the Nuba: they still dress in the traditional fashion, with no more than a light blanket over the shoulder.

I held some formation courses among the Shilluk, who had not seen a priest for ten years. I did the same with the Nuba later. The very day I arrived, no sooner had I cleaned myself of the mud than I met a group of youth in the church. They had gathered for a refresher course of a month's duration. Their faces betrayed trepidation. I asked them what they expected from the course. One of them said:

"*Abuna*, I have never attended a course given by a priest. My knowledge of the Christian faith is limited to the essentials. You must have come to tell us something very important. What I expect is not as important as what you have to tell us. I am ready to learn."

Daniel's faith struck me. Not only did he have faith in God, but also he trusted me. He had not met me personally, but in me he saw those missionaries who for 100 years had sacrificed themselves to evangelise his people. The missionaries who loved them, had spent the best part of their lives among them. They had died there, and were buried in the small cemetery next to the church. Their names on the cement crosses are hardly legible, not only because of the wear and tear of time, but also because of the bullets that had disfigured them in the course of many a battle. But they are there, silent witnesses to everlasting love. Daniel could see them all, behind the strange priest standing before him.

Cemeteries Under the Nile

On Good Friday 1996 I was back in Tonga. As I had done before, I returned with a load of basic medicines for a Shilluk medical doctor supported by an Italian NGO. A swarm of children immediately surrounded me, and accompanied me along the cobblestones leading to the Nile. They showed me an incongruous "Brick Factory" sign, nailed to the trunk of a tree around which bricks used to be made and cooked for building the missions. There is even a canal that takes Nile water to the "factory." This canal was dug under the direction of Joshua dei Cas, a holy man who contracted leprosy at Tonga and was allowed by his Comboni superiors to wait for death among his African friends. He died in the leprosarium of Kormalan, more to the south, in 1934. The soil all around the mission is bare. In 1984 the government army, besieged by the SPLA, cut down all the great mango trees planted by the missionaries to prevent the advancing army from taking cover behind them.

A ten minute walk separates the Nile from the mission. On the way one crosses a small cemetery, where only two graves are still visible. One is Sr Dominique Cereghini's, with a gravestone half in Shilluk and half in Italian. She died in 1954 after 33 years of uninterrupted missionary work among the Shilluk. The other is Bro. Remigius Zappella's, a missionary from early youth. There is hardly anything about him in the Comboni archives in Rome. It appears that he was in Aswan in 1903, and thereafter in Tonga. But the mission's diary has a long excerpt about him. On 15th December 1933 he was taken ill. The entry for the 24th says:

Bro. Remigius died this morning at 5:30 a.m. He was fully conscious to the last moment, and received the last Sacraments. He was buried in the afternoon of the same day in the presence of all the Christians. Brother Remigius was a missionary of crystal-clear character, innocent of duplicity. His physique was as strong as his spiritual life.

I was asking myself: "Where are the successors of those early missionaries today?"

The local catechist had prepared the rite for the Adoration of the Cross. The church was full of women and children, plus a dozen men. The war, hatred and fanaticism had devastated the life of these people. They had stared at evil in the face. They had suffered it and done it too. Some of them had killed, other had raped and been raped, men as much as women. Others had tortured, or been tortured. From this perspective, 90 years of sacrifice by missionaries, catechists and committed laypeople looked like a complete waste of time. After the rite I asked a woman who could speak English: "Why are you Christian?" She barely hesitated before answering, with a smile: "I need salvation and the eternal life that Jesus gives."

One can see the faith standing out in this place. The buildings are in ruins, the development projects of the 1970s dead in their tracks, no formal religious instruction has been imparted for at least ten years. But the faith is very much alive in the hearts of the people. It is a strong and essential faith, without statues of weeping Madonnas, special devotions, learned explanations of the Social Doctrine of the Church or sophisticated debates on sexuality. There is a single certainty: Jesus is in the right, he has words of eternal life. And there is a strong, burning desire to be with Him, so much so that some people walked for two days to be at the Easter celebrations.

This is the church that gathers around the celebration of the Easter fire. There is a dignified old man with his facial initiation markings still distinct, the adolescent girl with her elaborated hairdo, the thin woman who brought me Nile water in the morning and that now looks like a queen, with a shining cloth over her right shoulder. We celebrate the Eucharist, sing, clap, tap the drums and blow a venerable brass trumpet that the old catechist keeps for the great occasions. All express joy at the resurrection of Jesus. There follows the baptism of 65 young adults and 164 babies. Their mothers hardly contain their joy and dance with their young ones, still dripping water from the generous amounts I poured over their heads. The afternoon heat, 47 degrees in the shade, is extreme, but no one cares. I feel outside time. Is this 1996? The presence of the past is stronger than the misery of the present. I feel at home, despite my being a total stranger, speaking not a word of the local language. But aren't we sent by God, lord of heaven and earth? The missionary, the Christian are at home wherever they go. We don't belong to this earth, but have the right to go everywhere.

When I preach or speak to people, I constantly realise the powerful impact of the Gospel on those with an open heart, like the Tonga people. We who are used to it, but not ready to be struck by it, behave as "religious professionals," turning the Gospel into a product matched by our mediocrity and poverty.

Next I visited Detwok, a mission on the Nile founded by Joseph Beduschi, a Comboni pioneer. It was December 7th, St Ambrose's feast day, the very saint to whom the mission had been dedicated. I found the site under water, owing to the motions of the Nile. I looked for the cemetery where Beduschi has been buried since 1924. His grave was half a metre under water. Inside an imposing church, complete with a crypt for meetings, I found a statue of Our Lady, headless and without hands, riddled with bullet scars as much as the mission walls, which had seen many battles.

This kind of pilgrimage to the graves of many old Comboni had taken me, in February 1996, to Santa Croce, the southernmost mission visited by Comboni in person. The idea had come to me in July 1995 on returning from Rumbek. I had started working for the diocese of Rumbek shortly before. I had proposed to make my visit on the day of Comboni's beatification. Fr Caesar Mazzolari, at the time the apostolic administrator of Rumbek, agreed to join me, combining the visit with the opening of another mission at Adior. But we decided to bring forward the trip by a few weeks, to make it possible to publish an article in the Italian magazine *Famiglia Cristiana* in time for the beatification of Comboni. We left with two cars from Mapourdit, in the company of the journalist who would write the article, and a few others. Our Sudanese guide had taken part in the 1972 Olympics in Munich, and was a great-grand-nephew of the chief of the area where the old mission stood.

Trouble struck early: one of the two Land Rovers got stuck while crossing an almost dry river bed. The trip was mad and seemed endless, more so because we were never certain of our bearing. We were treading ground where a 4-wheel drive had never been before; it was touch-and-go, coming back and retracing steps, crossing swamps and seeing incredible landscapes.

On arriving, towards evening, we were welcomed by a burst of machine-gun fire not a metre from our vehicle. We were right in the middle of a Dinka cattle-camp, manned by young men. Our guide alighted and identified himself. As he treated with the chiefs, we got streams of intrigued visitors surrounding our vehicle.

At ten pm we pitched our tent in the middle of nowhere, over a mixture of mud and cattle dung. Our dinner consisted of canned tuna eaten in a hurry by carlight, surrounded by clouds of mosquitoes. Goodnight. Next morning we saw a watery landscape dotted with islets of papyrus. We got to a cement beacon erected by the Combonis in 1936 on high (and dry) ground. Our guide explained: "Here was the house, here the cemetery, here the mooring for the boats…" We were standing on the place where some missionaries had lived almost 150 years before. It was the site of the village where they bought slaves to rescue them. The probable site of their burial was near. We found no remains of the mission, which we had not expected to find, since it had been built for temporary purposes. Some in our group expressed doubts that we were on the right site. Our guide was indignant: "People here hardly see visitors for a lifetime. Do you entertain doubts that they would not be able, for years to come, to indicate the place where you five *khawaja* pitched your tent last night?"

In Santa Croce lie the remains of four missionaries: Louis Pircher of Trent, d. 1856; Bartholomew Mosgan of Maribor (Croatia) and Francis Oliboni of Verona, d. 1858; and James Kofler of Bressanone, d. 1861. They were young people who did not hesitate to lay down their lives for Africa. Mosgan, the older, was not 35 at his death. He had founded the mission four years earlier, among the Kic clan of the Dinka. On 14th February 1858, three weeks after Mosgan's death, six missionaries disembarked from the *Stella Matutina*. Comboni was one of them, as was Isidore Zilli, a layman. They began to work hard: in less than a month they had a 3.000 word dictionary. But on March 26th Oliboni said farewell.

> Dear Brethren, I'm dying. I am happy, as it is God's will. Do not get discouraged. Never give up, even though only one of you should remain. I am certain that God wants this African mission and the conversion of the Africans. I die with this absolute certainty…

They were prophetic words. Shortly the group was undone. Some were struck by fever, others had to be repatriated to Verona. Comboni alone stayed put. A Cardinal of Propaganda Fide had dubbed him "a madman deserving to be tied with 14 chains."

On 15th January 1859 even the surviving missionaries had to return to Khartoum. They were joined by those from Gondokoro on the Upper White Nile. The climate, bad health, Arab and white slave traders conspiring against them, and the suspicious and negative attitude of the Bari and the Kic had convinced them of the impossibility to continue. Shortly afterwards Comboni too, racked by fever, had to return to Italy, to set foot in Sudan once again in 1865. But he never pushed as far south as that again. And the Santa Croce mission was never reopened, apart from a weak, though generous, attempt two years later. His dying words (10th October 1881) were "Santa Croce and Gondokoro!"

After a brief ceremony we planted a large metal cross – made of water pipes carried all the way from Nairobi – on the site of the cemetery. We would have stayed longer, but apart from Santa Croce's inhospitableness, it was a war zone. It was an intense moment, of thanksgiving and remembrance.

But the Kau-Nyaro were calling. In December of that same year I made another attempt at reaching them on foot from the south. As it was Shilluk territory, I had contacted Lam, who had sent word ahead and advised me to start in mid-December, "When the marshes dry up, otherwise you won't be able to walk." Luckily that year had not rained much. I got there by air on a CCM aircraft bringing provisions to one of their doctors in Aburok. Lam Akol had placed 30 men and their commander at my disposal. We had a 120km march before us. Lam instructed them: "You are responsible for Fr Kizito's security. He decides whether to proceed or not. But in case of military emergencies you take the necessary decisions." We left with enthusiasm. But the swamps were anything but dry! It was an absurd journey, the worst I have ever undertaken in the Sudan, dragging myself along with mud up to my waist... Then I was apprehensive about snakes, insects, animals of all types, and billions upon billions of flies and mosquitoes. It is the terrible environment of the Nile from Juba to Malakal, where water flows, so to speak, over a gradient of 3 centimetres to a kilometre. Seneca heard its description from two centurions who had undertaken to find the sources of the Nile on Nero's orders. He transcribed it in his *Quaestiones Naturales*:

After many days we reached immense marshes. Not even the locals knew the exits, and no one else can ever hope of finding them: the weeds were forming thick mats, forming an impenetrable barrier both for travellers on foot and on a boat, because the slimy surface of the swamp hardly allows a small boat with one man to float.

It was the Sudd.

We were getting away from that swamp. On the third day the situation clearly improved, but it was obvious that I could not make it to my destination, stop there and return in good time to board the returning aircraft. Dog-tired and demoralised, I decided to turn back and make a new attempt in February, when the ground would definitely be drier. I left to Lam Akol, seeds, hoes and other utensils. A month later he succeeded in getting the cases to Kau, confirming that I could try again whenever I wanted. But immediately afterwards the zone was attacked by the government and subtracted from Akol's control. It was no longer possible to go to Kau. At the end of 2002 I broached the subject again. Lam sternly recommended me not to go: "Kau and Nyaro no longer exist. War and the drought have scattered the people. Some scouts I sent reported that there is nobody there." But as people reacquired confidence after the ceasefire of 19th Jaunary 2002, things began to change and people started to return home. Perhaps another attempt would bear fruit.

Kuwa the Rebel

The Arabs want the Nuba lands because the North is a desert. Here there are plains, especially near Heiban, which can grow cotton, sorghum, and where tractors can be used... they needed those lands and therefore had to expel the Nuba.

Thus spoke a Nuba journalist of the new generation, explaining the genesis of the war. Stephen Amin Arrno, third of six children, was born in El Obeid in 1976, after his parents' move from the Otoro hills to Khartoum. He studied at the Comboni College there, and then in Nairobi where he graduated in social communications.

He says that he discovered his people by reading the weekly *Sunday Nation* in my office. He would see the place of his roots in my company. Let him describe the impact.

We were going towards Kauda, when we met a group of women who gave us water to drink. Speaking to them, I discovered that one of them was an aunt of mine. She cried, we embraced... and she ran to alert the whole family. I saw my grandfather for the first time. And I asked myself: 'How is it possible that I have been denied the right to know my family?' I said to myself that I did not want to end up like them: the Nuba get the most degrading work. Even my parents had been engaged in very humble tasks. I didn't want that, I wanted to be proud to be a Nuba, just as a German is proud to be a German, and an Italian an Italian. From that day on, to be a Nuba for me has meant to help my brethren Nuba to discover our culture, and to be proud of it without bowing our head before other cultures that have clipped our wings and castrated our mind.

The war broke out then for economic reasons. The best Nuba lands were invaded by Arabs wanting to introduce mechanised agriculture. Agribusiness had the effect of reducing the area of the traditional Baggara pastures, who invaded Nuba lands with their herds. Conflict started between farmers and herders. "Court cases were resolved in favour of the Baggara and against the Nuba," as historian Douglas Johnson remarks without mincing words.[14]

There is also a cultural motive behind the war: the increasing pressure to obliterate Nuba culture by Arabising it. Stephen explains:

I am sorry to say, but one of the reasons why the Nuba are badly tolerated and persecuted is the spreading of Islam in its most intolerant version imposed on Sudan. It clashes with African culture, it does not respect it, and wants to annihilate it at all costs. Take the dress for instance: they want everybody, even children, to go well covered. And they do not respect at all the figure of the *kujur*, the healer.

Abdelaziz, Kuwa's early associate, has more details about the reasons behind the decision to take up arms. "At the University of Khartoum, a Nuba group founded the Komolo association. Its aim was to struggle for the rights of the Nuba with peaceful means. Kuwa's project was to infiltrate the institutions and that part of government controlled by the Socialist Sudan Union, particularly around Nimeiry, get elected and try to change things as MPs. Our aims were simple, like building schools and improving health institutions... After graduation, Yousif started teaching in a high school at Kadugli.

We tried to dissuade him, both because a teacher's salary was not much, and without money one does not achieve anything, and because what could he do for us from Kadugli? But he replied, "I'm not interested in money and a fat salary. I want to change society. I want to organise the youth. At Kadugli he quickly became popular, both in school and out of it. He liaised with Nuba people at all levels, stressing that their children were his pupils. He met with intellectuals as much as with workers coming to Kadugli as casuals. At every holiday he went to the interior to see his family,

[14] Douglas H. Johnson, *The Root Causes of Sudan's Civil Wars,* James Currey, Oxford 2003 p. 132.

neighbours and friends old and new. That's how he improved his knowledge of the Nuba world.

In 1981 Nimeiry set up regional parliaments. People urged Yousif to run for a seat. Without means, Yousif campaigned on foot and by bicycle, instructing and organising. He was the best at such activities. Kuwa was elected to the Kordofan Regional Assembly, located at El Obeid.

The clash with the supporters of the government was not long in coming. Bushara, the arrogant governor, could not swallow the fact that Kuwa challenged the executive in the House. But Kuwa was only telling the truth when pointing out that the whole of Nuba land was being neglected, and that development initiatives were needed there. Such frankness was appreciated in the House, even by the Baggara representatives. But the government hated him and threats began. At the slightest disturbance in Nuba land, even the smallest students' strike in the remotest corner of the region, the governor accused Kuwa. "The culprit is Kuwa the rebel." The situation was becoming increasingly tense. One of Kuwa's colleagues, a sort of regional minister, invited Kuwa to his home: "Yousif, your continued public clashes with the governor are unbecoming for you. Avoid them for the sake of the Nuba and your own." "But why?" "You see, Kuwa. Even when praying, one at times pronounces the verses of the Qur'an aloud, at other times *sotto voce*. The governor had suggested to the minister approaching Yousif and inducing him to moderation. He continued: "If you annoy the government you'll get into trouble. Why don't you go to the governor's house? His doors are always open. If you wish I can organise a meeting, and you will be able to explain your worries to him." "But what I want is to be listened to by all!"

Yousif went his way, facing a thousand dangers including the withdrawal of parliamentary immunity. He was risking prison. But he was undeterred, eventually joining the SPLM/A.

The situation worsened by the day, especially after Khartoum began to arm the militia. One day the Arabs raided and killed 60 000 heads of cattle in Dinka territory, after which they seized two great Nuba water reservoirs to irrigate their lands. The Nuba protested, first because the Dinka, left without cattle, would soon come to raid them to restock their herds; and second because they needed the water for their herds, not to irrigate Arab land. Arab arrogance was backed by automatic weapons. They killed seven Nuba. The Nuba regrouped with their traditional weapons, but the match was uneven. The policeman in charge of managing the situation was a Nuba, but he sided with the Arabs. The Nuba sent a delegation to El Obeid to see Yousif. Kuwa went straight to the governor, who ignored the reality on the ground and accused him once more of fostering instability.

The tension rose, until other MPs came to Yousif's defence. One of them invited him to the Ramadhan celebration. After sunset, sated with food, Yousif laid dozing on a mattress. But he overheard a conversation to the effect that arms and ammunition were to be distributed to the Baggara and to the local chiefs. He feigned sleep while listening to the end of the conversation. The governor was behind the plot. Kuwa realised that the war was no longer against the South as a whole, but against the Nuba particularly. And he began seriously to consider forming an army to defend the Nuba, even joining an existing armed group. He began throwing out feelers, both at Kadugli and Khartoum. One day he approached Abdelaziz proposing him to meet "a rebel." At the first contact with the SPLA, in 1984, the rebel turned out to be Edward Lino, liaison officer in the Bahr el Ghazal. They met him at Khartoum. Yousif told the Komolo group about the decision to enter the armed struggle, and Komolo put him in charge of getting in touch with the rebel headquarters and their leader. The aim was to weigh the SPLA *Manifesto* against the aspirations of the Komolo. Yousif managed to get a visa to Nairobi. Anyone applying for such a visa was suspect, since the government thought that the SPLA had its headquarters in Nairobi. A month later he wrote, saying that he had met Daniel Kodi and other leaders of the movement, and that he had read the *Manifesto*. "Know that you are now part of the SPLA." It was November 1984.

Abdelaziz is the witness of what the jump into the armed struggle meant for Kuwa and the others, who up to that moment had opted for democratic methods. For him, a politician who believed in peacefully settling questions, to take up arms was a very hard decision. But the choice was taken after a long frustrating experience. Yousif had already tried to seek a solution through the Sudan Socialist Union (SSU) of President Nimeiry. But there was no more room for compromise with that regime. To watch from the sidelines was no longer possible. The "wait and see" approach had to be replaced with a clear statement of position. They had even thought of infiltrating the SSU at local level, trying to influence government decisions into developing their areas. This approach worked at Kadugli, where they had won the elections and controlled the SSU; but the government realised it and isolated the local party branch. It refused to implement any resolution by the branch. Then they thought of raising the sights by entering the fledgling regional parliament, where Yousif got a seat. But even there they were not able to attain their aims. And when some members were sent to the National Parliament, their questions were answered with opposition and threats, even of death. They had exhausted all the peaceful, democratic means, which had been resounding failures. Even with the existence of a parliament, the real situation was that of a civil dictatorship. Whoever sat on the Presidential chair was a true dictator *de facto*.

Rebellion, after all, was nothing new. Fr Philip Ghabboush had started one in 1964 against the British-inspired poll tax. The Nuba refused to pay it. Yousif, as member of the Nuba General Union, took part in it. Armed groups attacked the police and the civil administration. The army had to intervene. Stephen, in primary school at the time, also took part, wielding a stick hunting for a certain government representative. The police managed to disperse them.

Heiban saw another revolt in 1969. The Moro and the Otoro took up arms protesting against the Nimeiry coup. The Army immediately marched on Kadugli to disperse the popular movement.

Fr Philip got in touch once more with the Anya-nya I, and joined it with some 30 young Nuba. When the peace negotiations of 1972 were signed, Ghabboush rejected them. In 1975 there was an entire company, of some 100-110 men, led by Yousif Mubarak, a Moro, who joined the Anya-nya II, those who had not signed the negotiations of 1972.

1982 saw another armed insurrection. This time it was by a group of exiles from that company. There were six or seven fatalities and some 30 wounded among government troops. The Nuba had revolted three times against the British, so that the 1984 decision to take up arms did not come out of the blue. All Yousif did was to continue a tradition. The decision was not personal. As a leader he tried to assess the situation, interpreting the mind of the people and deciding what direction to take.

A Jihad Against Fellow Muslims

ccording to a 1995 report by the NGO African Rights, war began in Nuba territory in 1985.[15] The Nuba did not start military operation then, but two events triggered off the war. The first was the SPLA "Dinka" foray in southern Kordofan, and the second, the government's decision to fully arm a Baggara group. Their attacks on the Nuba were not delayed for long, increasing in frequency and violence. The situation, already deteriorating, had convinced Kuwa to opt for the armed struggle.

The Komolo group had kept an eye on the SPLA ever since the latter's inception.

> We were convinced that the SPLA was the right political mechanism that would allow us to attain our political aims, i.e. Nuba self-determination.

Kuwa spoke those words to Stephen Amin for Africanews, a press agency born in our *Koinonia* community. On his return from Cuba in 1986, Kuwa was sent to Bonga, Ethiopia, at the head of the Volcano battalion. After a few months training, he led his men to the Nuba Mountains, with the idea of recruiting local forces. Kuwa had immediately been co-opted into the SPLA High Command. He noticed that he had been "highly considered" in the Movement from the beginning.

---

[15]   *Facing Genocide: The Nuba of Sudan.* It is a fundamental text for the history of the genocide on the Nuba Mountains.

Kuwa, though a fully-fledged military commander, was different. Abdelaziz mentions how frank and direct he was. With his teaching background, he was always ready to correct people. He wanted to be a reformer, and wanted around him honest people who would not lie. Liars he would send them away, as happened to many. At the same time he was very kind and sensible. Abdelaziz narrates:

> When I travelled to the South for my military training, Yousif was arriving from Addis Ababa. The place was dirty and we were unkempt, but he was well dressed. On seeing the soldiery in such conditions, he went to the Gambela market and personally bought some insecticide. Then he ordered: "Get me the Nuba." There were 14 or 15 of us. He gave us to eat: "I'm sure you're hungry." He had also bought razor blades for us. He cared for everyone.

Although his commander's status was undisputed, he always tried dialogue in order to convince. It was very different from the usual military style. On one occasion, on the Nuba Mountains, a southern officer started giving trouble, talking to all and sundry to the effect that he wanted to return home "to my children," as he put it. Then he tried another card with Yousif, alleging that he was sick and in need of cure. Yousif, very calm, answered:

"If you are that sick, the distance is such that you could die on the way. I will send someone to Bentiu to fetch medicines... but if you insist, go."

Abdelaziz sent the man away and blurted out:

"Do you allow him to do what he wants? He's having us on."

"No, I want to believe him."

Abdelaziz was embarrassed and annoyed at the man's running away. But Yousif explained:

"If one is not fully convinced he should work for us, it's no use keeping him. He would not be of any help."

Yousif's education and experience made him behave like a statesman, or like a father more than a soldier. This attitude made it possible for him to keep control of the Nuba Mountains, rather than just the military actions.

Early in 1989 Yousif returned to the Nuba Mountains at the head of six battalions of the New Kush division. The bulk of the troops were Nuba. Meanwhile the Baggara *murahaliin* and government troops were continually raiding the villages, alleging SPLA presence there (which was true although sporadic).

Alex de Waal and Yoannes Ajawin, writing for African Rights, reported:

> On 28th May 1988 a big government contingent moved to Kalala and Jebel Nukri. In two weeks they burned and razed 21 villages. It was an utter devastation. They abducted people, thirteen of whom we know. They set fire to all Christian chapels, but not to the mosques, which at the time they left intact. Luckily there were only eleven casualties. Almost all the inhabitants went to hide in caves. During the rainy season they trusted that the army would not come back, so they started rebuilding their homes. But after the rains the raids restarted. On 25th September an Arab militia attacked the Omo village. They would apply the same strategy in the Darfur in 2003-2004. It was genocide in both places.

The use of the term "genocide" has become controversial. On the one hand it is applied to any type of massacre, and on the other withdrawn when it would be uncomfortable to use it. There is in fact a UN convention "for the prevention and repression of the crime of genocide." It happened in Rwanda in 1994. The Clinton Administration engaged in a worldwide promotion of the movie *Schindler's List* by Spielberg and the Jewish holocaust; while at the same time the American representative in the UN Security Council took no notice of the genocide taking place in the heart of the African continent. African Rights was fully conscious of the juridical meaning of the term, which is "intention to destroy a group as such." They did not hesitate to apply it to the Nuba region, in both cultural and physical sense:

> If the Sudan government is allowed to apply its policies without being stopped for a year or two, the final balance will be thousands of Nuba killed, the greater part of women and girls raped, children separated from their parents and forced to change their identity. Apart from the tens of thousands killed, the survivors will not be identifiable as Nuba.

They will be politically subjugated and socially dismembered; their culture will be annihilated.

De Waal and Ajawin were writing the above ten years into the war.

Millard Burr, a consultant of the United States Committee for Refugees (USCR) made some calculations for both the Nuba Mountains and southern Sudan.[16] Up to 1988 some 200 000 Nuba had disappeared, out of an estimated population of 1.5 million. Another 100 000 had been deported to northern Kordofan, 172 000 to so-called "peace camps", many tens of thousands forcibly recruited into the army or the militia, or sent as refugees to Khartoum and Port Sudan. The estimates are short of the mark. The Nuba under SPLA administration are now more than 400 000.

The government escalated the confrontation between 1991 and 1992. The first measure was to block all ingoing and outgoing trade from the Nuba Mountains, together with military operations that aimed at the destruction not only of homes and people, but also of markets, cultivated fields and food stocks. The populations, losing the means of subsistence, withdrew higher and higher on the Mountains, where fertile soils are scarce. In January 1992 Abdel Karim el-Hussein, the Governor General of southern Kordofan, declared a *jihad* on the Nuba. Obviously the power of Turabi's National Islamic Front (NIF) was being consolidated in Khartoum.

But many Nuba are Muslims, and a Jihad against co-religionists needed a theological justification. A specious *fatwa*,[17] issued in April at El-Obeid, branded as an "apostate" anyone either in South Sudan or in southern Kordofan who would join the insurgency against the State. The perfect syllogism followed: whoever is not a Muslim is an unbeliever, and Islam reserves to kill unbelievers and apostates. How much religious and/or political content there is in such reasoning is self evident. Young Mende Nazer had spotted the incongruence in her own way, the evening when the *mujaheddin* came to lay waste her village and take her into slavery:

---

[16] *Quantifying genocide in Southern Sudan and the Nuba Mountains, 1983-1988.*

[17] Authoritative juridical-religious opinion by an Islamic conference.

92

I was petrified. The words were those that my father uttered when slaughtering a goat or a fowl. If he had not dedicated the animal to Allah with that formula, in fact, it would not have been *halal*, i.e. purified and ready to be eaten. Why those men shouted *Allah akbar* after having set the village on fire, raped and killed? Did they believe that this sort of behaviour was *halal?* We were Muslims like them.

When we came to know, from Douglas Johnson's quote earlier, that in March 1993 the government announced the sale of nine agricultural areas on the Nuba Mountains, receiving 40 000 offers from Arab entrepreneurs, the cycle closes.

One of the instruments behind this policy was the peace camps. In June-July of that same year at least 30 000 Nuba were interned in these true concentration camps. They were made use of as cheap labour, and forcibly circumcised. The women were taken as "temporary" wives by Muslim soldiers, in a clear intent of ethnic cleansing and forced genetic change. The children, which made up 80% of the residents of those "villages" were separated from their families and employed practically as slaves. They were forced to attend schools with compulsory Qur'an teaching in the official version of Islam. Any access route to the Nuba Mountains had been sealed. The international humanitarian organisations had to keep distances, even during the famine of 1993. The exceptions were few and far between. Operation Lifeline Sudan was never authorised by the government to intervene in SPLA-controlled areas.

Farid came from one of these camps. Musa Kuwa, Yousif's brother, brought him to me after receiving him in turn from NRRDO, the Nuba Relief Rehabilitation and Development Organisation of the Nuba. Together with Farid was another tiny boy called Yohannes, so small that was never able to relate what had happened to him. Farid told his story. One day, as he was working in the fields at the bottom of a valley, with his parents (his young siblings had been left half way up the mountain) and other farmers, a government column arrived, got hold of them and tried to abduct them all. They succeeded in grabbing some. The father had resisted and tried to escape; he was stopped and killed in cold blood as an example. They were all taken to a peace camp, where his mother was forced to be the concubine of one of the officers and Farid sent to work in a field, practically a slave. After a couple of years the mother died of tuberculosis, judging by Farid's description. He and two or three more managed to escape. He returned to his land, but the village had disappeared. None of his siblings had survived. NRRDO found him in that situation and brought him to us. The two are today at Anita House, one of the initiatives of Koinonia in Nairobi. That's what peace camps were like.

When Julie Flint shot a documentary film for the BBC, she traced, outside Sudan, a repentant commander of a peace camp. She asked:

"What were you authorised to do to those who tried to escape?"

"Anything we wanted."

Alec Saleh's answer was matter-of-fact.

The *jihad* caught the resistance in a moment of crisis. A crop had been lost. Riek Machar and Lam Akol had split from Garang's SPLA (Kuwa stuck with him so as not to remain politically isolated) and they lacked arms just when the government had deployed 40 000 men with heavy artillery and air support. Arms captured from the enemy were not enough.

Kuwa organised an expedition to Bahrel-Ghazal to fetch ammunition. It was the epic enterprise of 400 soldiers, during the dry season, thirsty and having to battle their way there. 240 of them died. A second attempt was made in July during the wet season, when fighting is necessarily suspended. But the marshes and stagnant waters accounted for another 100 of the best men of the New Kush division. Kuwa announced that he could not bear the brunt of the responsibility single-handed. Rather than resigning, which he would have in normal circumstances, he decided to convoke a general assembly. 110 delegates met at Debi on 10th October 1992, defying the risk of long transfers and consequent exhaustion. They were almost all civilians, representing the Nuba before the SPLA. Kuwa accepted responsibility for all the problems arising from what had happened. He was ready to hand over so as to avoid their being repeated. He would help in handing over. But it was the assembly that had to decide whether to carry on the war or not. Urged on by the women present, Yousif was reconfirmed in power unanimously, with only eleven votes against.

Furthermore, his experience of democratic practice led him to convoke a convention of the whole SPLM/A, to listen to dissident opinion and to discuss what forms a civil administration in the liberated zones should take. Kuwa himself presided over the preparatory commission, and later over the assembly held at Chukudum. John Garang himself, talking into Julie Flint's microphone, acknowledged that Kuwa "respected religion, race and gender... He had shown how to do it on the Nuba Mountains, he could therefore repeat the feat for the whole of the SPLA."

Yousif returned to his hills in 1995, after almost two years. When he saw his people, he could not hold back his tears.

At that time I too began to tread Nuba paths.

Everybody to School

J had been walking for almost three hours, back from a visit to Dr Ziyada, who for the past three years had been practicing medicine on the Nuba Mountains. We walked by moonlight, and the sun was just rising when we could see the summits on one side and the vast plain on the other, barely visible through the mist. The three of us started climbing along a ridge, when we suddenly saw our destination, Kachama Primary School. It was located on a flat piece of ground protected by a bluff of rock. Buildings were of mud and thatch. The place was already humming with activity.

Hundreds of kids were rushing to school in time for the roll call. Further on, the ground sloped steeply into another piece of flat ground. In the far distance one could see the sunrays reflected by numerous mabati roofs. We were looking at Heiban, the second largest town after Kadugli in Nuba land. It was under government control, whereas the school was in an SPLA liberated area.

An image of the Blessed Virgin Mary in an attitude of prayer had been painted on the only smooth wall. The caption, in Arabic, said: "The Church unites all people, and all are children of God." There were 717 students. Schooling is free. The pupils eat the only meal in the afternoon, but they are already hungry on reaching school after an hour's walking early in the morning. The 18 teachers are all volunteers. The greater part are catechists, or in charge of communities belonging to various Christian denominations in the surrounding villages. None are trained teachers.

I walked from classroom to classroom, asking questions of students and teachers. I was impressed by their enthusiasm for study and their courage before the obvious difficulties. The students were a mixed bunch of Christians, Muslims and traditionalists, and I realised the falsity of the standard charge according to which the war in Sudan has its origin in religious differences. I admired the wisdom and tolerance of the teachers. Without formal training, they were the graduates of the University of Life. Contrary to those who think that humankind would be better off without religion in a world where warring parties identify with their respective creed, here religion was a reason for unity and harmony.

I asked Zakariah Noh, the 30-something head teacher, the founder of the school, whose idea it had been. "Ours, the community elders'" he replied. "We wanted education for our children. Traditionally the responsibility for education falls on the grownups of the community. If I see a boy misbehave, I can upbraid him, and his father will support me. We are all interested in the development of our young people. So we asked anyone with knowledge to come forward and place his intellectual baggage at the service of the community."

At 11 o'clock the pupils left. "The Antonov bombers always arrive about noon" Zakariah explained. "We don't want to offer them an easy target. The pupils are safer at home, scattered all over the mountains." But 200 students, a group of teachers and people from the nearby homes were ready to risk. They stayed for Mass. I felt privileged to be their "father."

The date was November 1997. I reflected that those students were lucky to have such devoted volunteer teachers, perhaps not too fluent in the English language that they tried to impart them, but certainly in a position to educate with their lives, their love for freedom and justice, with their determination to be respected as human beings and their commitment for the common good. But at the same time they too needed a more solid formation.

I was thinking like that while eating an extremely abundant, unforgettable fruit salad of bananas, goavas and mangoes served in a split kalabash (they knew that I hardly ever eat meat). Just at that moment Joseph Aloga, one of the catechists that had guided me on the Nuba mountains, arrived, rather distraught, bearing a message from Kauda, where the SPLA receiver had got it from Nairobi. Andrew Awuor, 26, the *Koinonia* treasurer and director of Africanews, an extremely talented man, was in hospital victim of a road accident. The message urged me to return at once.

I left without delay. We stopped at Luere for a three-hour rest, after which we went down to Kauda in full moonlight. We stopped by the German Emergency Doctors, the only humanitarian organisation in the area with *Koinonia*. They were at Luere after a close shave with fighting at Kauda. At 1am we began the long climb to Gidel, but a couple of kilometres after Kauda we were startled by a red flare shooting up from a hill no more than 150 metres from us. I was petrified. Joseph froze.

- What's that, Joseph?
- I don't know.
- Is it SPLA?
- No. SPLA don't have such things.

It was doubtless a government patrol around Kauda. For years the game between SPLA and the government consisted in instilling fear to each other. Did the flare mean "we've seen you, go away," or were there more soldiers around? We hid, crouched, for a while. Then we started again up to the crest, crossing difficult passes where we knew that government soldiers didn't like to tread. Nothing happened until Gidel. I counted on reaching the nearest airstrip, three hours walking away, in time to board a 9am. flight to Lokichoggio. But at Gidel I found Julie Flint, whom I had not met before. She informed me: "No flights today."

I spent the whole endless day without knowing what was going on in Nairobi. It was November 18th. Andrew was dying. I promised myself that if Andrew died we would found a school in his memory. I returned to Nairobi with that resolution in my heart. After Andrew's death, Stephen Amin appeared on the scene from nowhere. He had frequented one year of journalism, but had run out of

98

scholarship money. I helped him to pay for his second year and got acquainted better. With Michael Owiso, in charge of *Amani People's Theatre*, the three of us organised an English crash course of three months in abandoned buildings at Kauda. The course took place between August and October 1998. But a bombing raid killed one of the students. He was running away as bombs were falling. A piece of shrapnel severed his left arm and he bled to death.

The course was so successful that next year we repeated it at Kerker, and in 2000 at Kujur Shabia. At the beginning of 2001, with money from the French *Sécours Catholique*, from the Amani Association and from others, we set up something permanent: the Kerker pilot school, in Rashad County. The land for teachers' housing was donated by the local mosque.

Kuwa, meanwhile, as a veteran teacher and having himself opened dozens of small schools (some 30 in Nagorban County) was looking upon these exertions with satisfaction and hope. He supported our idea of introducing English as if it had been his own. In October 2001, after his death, Abdelaziz met with the leaders of the Movement and those in charge of education. The choice was confirmed as one of cultural policy. Switching education from Arabic to English had a clear innuendo: it was a curt rejection of the Arabising policy of the government. Abdelaziz came to see me after that meeting with a handwritten document. He asked Koinonia

- To open a teacher training centre, since they were unable to manage the one they themselves had opened a few months earlier;
- To open a school like that at Kerker in every county under SPLA control: Rashad, Kadugli, Lagawa, Dilling, Nagorban, Delami, Buram and Heiban.
- To take on little by little the task of Nuba Ministry of Education.

I replied to Abdelaziz to forget points 2 and 3. For the teacher training we could try." The first yearly course for teachers took off at the Teacher Training Institute "Yousif Kuwa" at Gidel, not far from Kerker. The classrooms and dormitories for boys and for girls were constructed by the students themselves with local material.

What schooling means to a Nuba can be understood from the following story. It was May 1999. I had just landed at Gidel with a TV troupe, and the welcome was terrific: there were speeches, the latest news and details of the situation, and in the afternoon Nuba wrestling, dancing, singing, etc. Every group performed.

Suddenly I felt a tug on my shirt. It was a boy of about ten, haggard, dirty and with reddish hair from vitamin deficiency.

"Paolino! Where have you come from?"

"From Lomon."

Lomon is a mountain location where people had run to from the Teberi plains, to escape government raids. I had met the boy in his village, some 90 km away from where we were. I had not returned there since early 1998. Landing had become impossible because of government shelling. Paolino was a neighbour of Jibril Tutu, a Nuba apostle, and he had served my Mass on a number of occasions.

"How did you get here, Paolino?"

"With the soldiers."

"Why have you come?"

"To ask you to make me study. I want to be a catechist, and then a doctor."

Paolino spoke almost perfect English, perhaps rehearsed many times during his fourteen hours of walk. Many soldiers had walked to the reception from all over the Nuba Mountains, and he with them. I asked myself: "What do I do now? I can't disappoint him." I played for time.

"OK Paolino, I will see what I can do. But it is rather difficult, you know. So many things are necessary, documents and what not..."

But I told Musa Kuwa, in charge of Koinonia logistics, to take note of that boy. One evening in Nairobi I spoke about him at a meeting of the Koinonia Community. Michael Ochieng and his wife Jane Wamunga were there. She was the first "mama" of the Anita Home for street girls. They looked at each other.

"Father, bring him here. We have adopted eight girls in our family. One more will not change anything."

Jane spoke, unaware that a stroke would end her life, at 30, in May 2002. Paolino came to Nairobi. But what about all the others?

The first school year at Kerker "pilot school" was postponed to Easter 2001. Sporadic attacks had counselled not to have large gatherings of boys. At the end of April, Marko Lesukat, the Kenyan in charge of the enterprise, remained at Kerker with a pair of teachers and teaching material. As I was about to return we were bombed. Towards the end of May the government army went on the offensive, coming frighteningly close to the village. All the children ran away. The teachers and Marko escaped at night, crossing the Komo valley in great danger, since it was full of government troops, and sought shelter at Kujur Shabia, the safest place in the zone. A week later there was a mini truce. We evacuated Marko to Lokichoggio, but he refused to go back to Nairobi: he intended to return to Kerker on the first occasion. The school has grown thanks to the dedication of local people and of personnel we sent from Kenya. Despite many difficult moments, the project can be considered a success.

Marko's personal history is also worth telling. When deciding to open Kerker, I had counted on Ramadan Orandi's headmastership. I had met him in Nairobi, where he was studying management. Towards the end of 2000 Yousif Kuwa, who had only three months to live, called me:

"Father, I'm very sorry, but we absolutely need Ramadan. The SPLA offices in Kampala are in a mess, and we need someone to restore order there."

"What about us and the pilot school? Take Ramadan if you wish, but do you have someone else for the school?"

"No."

The main problem of the Nuba Mountains has always been the dearth of competent personnel. Whereas among the Dinka living in Nairobi one out of every two is a graduate, among the Nuba there isn't any, repeat any. I didn't know what to do. One day someone knocked. I opened the door to face a very tall young man.

101

"Do you remember me?"

"Not really."

"You came to our campus, showed us a video about the Nuba, towards the end of 1996."

"I had just started Engineering. When the documentary ended I came to you and said: "When I graduate I want to go and work on the Nuba Mountains.""

I remembered. During my ten years as university chaplain I had met this brilliant young man, who was the head of the Catholic students on campus. The young man went on:

"I am Marko Lesukat. I graduated yesterday. Here I am, ready to go to work in the Nuba Mountains."

Marko is of mixed ethic heritage. His mettle is unique. While herding goats as a boy, a Consolata missionary spotted his intelligence and helped him with his studies. He began primary school at twelve, and at 26 took his first degree in agricultural engineering. Now he has a M.Sc. in hydraulic engineering. In mid-January 2001 he spent two months with us at the Kivuli community to get acquainted with our working style, and then went to Kerker.

He did sterling work there, as a true born leader. At the end of the 2003 school year the SPLA administration singled out the Kerker School as the best managed and with the best results. The school has effectively transformed the appearance of the area: almost all boys and girls speak English, and almost everybody goes to school. From 450 pupils at the beginning, the school has now 640 and growing, because the truce has convinced many families to return, and the school itself is a magnet of attraction. Marko has also set up a parents-teachers committee of some 20 people. The parents of the committee are elected by the families, and they have a say in important decisions like building new classrooms, etc. They have also opted for affirmative action in favour of the girls, traditionally the last to be sent to school. The school fee for every boy is ten kilogrammes of sorghum per year; for the first daughter it is half of that, and for the second onwards the fee is waived. The results of 2001 showed a single girl among the top three students of all classes; at the end of 2003 the girls were one third of the same total.

Class Six opened at Kerker in 2004, ahead of schedule, since the will to study is such that some students can jump a class. A UNICEF consultant inspector suggested setting up a course so as to promote everyone from Class Six to Eight. He remarked that besides the willingness to work, the children had an agile and fresh mind, and that they should not waste time. For the time being the SPLM/A, leaves people free to choose between the Uganda and the Kenya system, because it is easier to get school material from Nairobi than from Kampala. The systems are somewhat similar.

Finding teachers has been the most serious problem from the beginning. Finances were extremely scarce. Money to fly teachers to Kerker, to keep in touch with them and give them a minimum of goods and teaching instruments were very high. Yousif Kuwa found Uganda teachers ready to go to Kerker for $100 a month. It is not a big sum, but it is net of expenses. There's nothing to buy on the Nuba. The first six teachers therefore were Ugandans. Later, by increasing the salary to $200 and giving some extra benefits, Kenyans were enticed into going. It is true that the salary is paid regularly, but still one needs a special spirit to be ready to spend a year non-stop at Kerker after coming from Nairobi. Some stay a whole year, but then they collect their savings and retire. One of them, still with a year and a half of university to go, signed a contract for the same duration, and with the money he finished his degree. Others have stuck it out for years, with a true spirit of service, establishing deep bonds of friendship with the Nuba. When they go, their idea is to come back later, after having established their position and continuing to serve... Marko was succeeded by Julius Odhiambo, with the same high Christian motivation.

Some teachers are Sudanese. Two of them grew up in refugee camps, at Kakuma or in Uganda, and came back to help their people to have education. Ugandans and Kenyans were recruited when there were no Nuba with formation, but our Gidel Institute is changing things fast. We also asked ourselves whether it would

103

not be worthwhile to recruit teachers from the liberated areas of the South, but Kuwa insisted on non-Arabic speakers, since Arabic was now the language of instruction in the new educational system of the Khartoum government. Experience had shown that Arab-speaking English teachers available at the time in Sudan, making use of Arabic as a medium of instruction, considerably retard learning.

English is taught not only to children but also to adults, with afternoon classes lasting until sunset. The number of English speakers is growing; one can find them almost everywhere. To change from Arabic to English, as propounded by Kuwa and continued by Abdelaziz, is a titanic endeavour. The target was to have 24 000 students with a certificate of primary education by 2005, all English speakers, taking into account that in SPLA-administered territory there are about 100 schools of all sizes. One may doubt the outcome, but not in the long run. 50 teachers a year graduate at Gidel, all qualified to teach well not only the English language, but also to make use of English in the teaching of other subjects at primary level. At Kauda the La Salle Language Institute of Minnesota runs shorter, three-month courses supported by Norwegian Church Aid, an ecumenical organisation. The process is accelerating. Soon there will no longer be need for many expatriates. It is good that a few should remain, especially as directors of the courses, as also one or two teachers in each school with a good command of English. The hour when all teachers will be Nuba is coming close. One of Gidel's aims is to graduate teachers able to form other teachers, after which our presence will no longer be required. It would seem that the Diocese of El Obeid will take charge of the schools, barring opposition from the government and from the Movement.

Meanwhile Koinonia is building new premises for Gidel, equipping them with a library, audiovisuals and solar-powered computers. This type of energy is already known on the Nuba Mountains, both for lighting teachers' houses and for powering the radios that link the three schools. The third school was built at

Kujur Shabia, in cooperation with NRRDO. It enjoys the undeniable advantage of security from lying at an altitude of 1070 metres, and therefore beyond the reach of land military operations. But there is little access to water and whatever is available is of poor quality. The solution will be to sink a well like the one sunk at Kerker after the opening of the school there.

In 2002 we opened Kujur Shabia with George Baridi as headmaster. He is a smart Kenyan, graduate in Education. He proved to be an excellent organiser, despite his former fame as a bookworm. He was chosen by a committee whose members are Stephen Amin, Ken Kanyanga and Richard Muko, in charge of selecting teachers for the Nuba schools. We travelled to Kujur Shabia with George and two teachers in August, during the rainy season. We introduced them to the people and left them there with a few books, miscellaneous items and one order, "Set up the school!" The situation would have made me shudder, but the real strength of Koinonia is its capacity towards mobilisation. Our great advantage is that the locals know me and the group. Returning in December, we found the project well on the way: teachers' lodgings were built and the classrooms were functioning. In three months the people had been fully motivated. The constructions are not posh, but neither are they miserable. The teaching personnel consist of seven Nuba and two Kenyans. And the headmaster is now Ramadan! They are intent on solving the water problem by means of a small dam and a well. People are ready to dig, because water is not too deep. The well needs topping with cement and being furnished with a pump. The cost is about $1 000. But the essential thing is to mobilise people, and Ramadan, a Nuba, is the ideal person to do it.

In January 2004 we struck gold. At the UNDP camp at Kauda, set up a few months earlier, I chanced to meet Wanjiru Githae, a dynamic Kenyan whom I readily convinced of the viability of our projects. She had personally realised the water problem at Kujur Shabia and the needs of the schools, and she respected Koinonia, a very small NGO, for having been present in the Nuba area when nobody else was. We started a useful collabration with UNDP.

Real Needs and Fake Slaves

Fundraising is a permanent need, but we often took the risk to start a project even without funds, when we tought it was needed, important. At Kujur Shabia, for instance, we began with a relatively small monetary support from Sign of Hope, a German organization for emergency help. For other projects the Italian Episcopal Conference as well as other Italian, Austrian, French, Irish and Spanish charities have contributed.

Our strength, as a friend who regularly visits Kivuli one day said, is that people find open doors, can come and see, and verify whether we solve problems or don't. Economic management is carried out at the level of the structures that Koinonia has set up little by little, with the support of Amani.

No take-off from Loki ever has an empty cargo hold. We sit on sacks and boxes full of school material, medicines, blankets, agricultural implements like the *maloda*, a characteristic hoe to scratch the hard Nuba soil. Of late we have been bringing cooking pots, to favour the resettlement of families that had run away during the war. But we never bring food. Kuwa, angry at times, had spoken clearly: "I don't want to create here the dependence that has been created in the South. In some areas there people sit and wait for aid, and no longer cultivate. Aid there kills local initiative and local markets."

In 1997 I took Kuwa to the Italian Embassy, to agree on an important project that Operation Lifeline Sudan would not touch, since its hands had been tied by their agreement with Khartoum. At the time any NGO acting outside the agreement between the government and OLS would have been expelled, as had Dr Meo from Pariang, which was an area outside the agreement. Therefore there was no international presence on the Nuba Mountains at the moment of the ceasefire – apart from the Germany Emergency Doctors, who with enormous courage and sacrifice kept a small hospital going from 1996 up to date, and us. Afterwards lots of them came, including a galaxy of American NGOs lavishly financed by the America state agency USAID, without looking at the strings attached to such funds.

On that day in 1997 the Italian Embassy agreed to support medical and agricultral needs, allocating a generous sum for the purpose. Everything went smoothly, except the initial insistence in sending food items together with medicines. Kuwa was adamant: "No, no, no. OK for the medicines, because we can't produce them. But we can produce all the food we need. Give us *maloda*, seed and salt. Iodine deficiency accounts for a high percentage of people with goitre, especially women."

Finally Kuwa managed to have his view accepted. He had a lot of respect for, and trust in the ability of the Nuba to be self-sufficient. He didn't want useless aid. He himself cultivated his vegetable garden whenever he could visit home. At Luere next to the hut where he lived and not far from his grave, there is still a pond for the ducks he had introduced there to start a small breeding farm. He liked novelties, provided that they stimulated local work. He was elated when I brought maize seeds of a drought-resistant variety, however small the quantity actually was.

In health matters, Koinonia supported Dr Hashim Ziyada for four years after 1995. After the Pariang misadventure he wanted to go to the Nuba Mountains. He considered the area as his own, since one of his parents was a Nuba. He was a graduate of John Hopkins University Baltimore. After graduating he had served in the Sudanese Health System, up to the rank of Health Inspector at El Fasher in the Darfur. Then he decided to join the SPLA. He travelled to Nairobi, contacted CCM and together with Dr Meo lived the Pariang adventure. Meo could have been freed earlier, but he insisted that the two of them be released together. They both travelled to Italy for a holiday, after which Ziyada declared he would like to work on the Nuba Mountains. Towards the end of 1995 he settled at the foothills of the Lomon Mountains. Six months later the place fell to the government. Ziyada commuted between Kauda and Luere, where he set up a small hospital. But age was taking its toll, and in 2000 he left for the South with a better organised NGO.

In 1997 a medical NGO, the already mentioned German Emergency Doctors settled in Kauda against Ziyada's and my advice, for the place was exposed to attack. In June 1998, in fact they had to take to their heels and rejoin Ziyada at Luere. They are still there, in turns. The hospital is built in stone, wood and thatch. The only difference with other constructions is the bustle of people coming and going, plus a few square metres of solar panels. The only luxury item in their residence is a darts game. The hospital averages 50 patients per day. The most frequent ailments are well known: malaria, dysentery, anaemia, worms, bronchitis and pneumonia. There are also STDs, but not too much AIDS. There is a maternity ward, separated from the main construction. The trouble is that when women in labour decide to go to hospital is because of incipient problems. When they arrive after a long journey, on a stretcher up and down mountain paths, it is generally too late.

Ziyada had managed to convince the Lokichoggio hospital, specialised in prostheses, to accept patients he would send by air. The tacit agreement was that at Loki they would pretend not to know that they hailed from the Nuba Mountains. The most common prostheses were required for legs or parts thereof blown off by mines, at times ten years before. Musa Kuwa was in charge, even after Dr Ziyada had left. Between 1999 and 2001 we took care of 60-65 casualties per year.

Kuwa gave in on the question of dress. When I began my trips on the Nuba Mountains, nakedness was almost absolute. The women wore nothing but a straw miniskirt, and the men, when they wore anything, it was patched-up, worn-out trousers. The people asked for clothes in payment for work, and Kuwa respected this need. As a respecter of tradition, for him shirts and trousers were unnecessary. But if it was the people that wanted to dress, tradition or no tradition, he let them. It is interesting to observe how much school girls care about the length of the skirt, and how they protest when that of the new uniform does not abundantly extend below the knee! The pressure on the part of the government towards dressing the Nuba has had its effect, albeit in other ways.

For everything else, like identifying needs and people in need, we ask NRRDO. It is the most obvious thing to do. At the beginning it consisted of just two people in charge of flight security. They would communicate via radio on whether landing was safe or not. In time it grew, and now it manages small projects and coordinates larger ones. Musa Kuwa, for instance, takes care of earth dams, eight of which have been rehabilitated and three new ones built.

NRRDO has more authority than foreign NGOs, since it is entirely Nuba. In October 1997 we took its director Naroun Philip Kuku to Italy, for a meeting with the Senate Foreign Commission. They also suffer for lack of competent personnel. NRRDO has a much weaker structure than SRRA (Sudan Relief and Rehabilitation Association), the relief arm of the SPLM/A. And despite the occasion for corruption, I have yet to hear of such in regard of NRRDO. Kuwa took care of such problems personally, so that he felt depressed when the first case of theft was reported. On the occasion of Lam Akol's first trip to Nairobi as Minister of Transport for South Sudan, he threw a party at Kibera. Neither Kuwa nor I went, because that very morning it had been discovered that a Nuba woman employee of the NRRDO office had stolen more than $30 000. Her story was that she had withdrawn the money from a bank (no one was authorised to do so without escort) and that someone had stolen it from her house. That money was never recovered. For NRRDO, which operated on an annual budget of some $150 000, that was a substantial loss.

There is never a lack of smart Alecs who take advantage of relief aid. The Sudanese quickly understood the rules of the game and conformed. At the beginning of the 1990s there were already local NGOs in charge of emergency, health, education and micro-credit, but in reality they were managed by Sudanese resident in Nairobi, in cahoots with the high ranks of the SPLM/A that gave jobs to friends and relatives. Thus did they make happy the international community, which had begun to discover "the representatives of civil society." These characters quickly became extremely accomplished in collecting funds. They also mastered the jargon of the humanitarian experts, and began making a lavish use of terms like *empowerment, gender balance, capacity building* etcetera, so as to be present in the circuit of seminars and working dinners held in Nairobi.

A particular case was the Christian Solidarity International (CSI). The director of this originally Swiss organisation was an American, John Eibner. In October 1996 he began moving in SPLA-controlled areas, in the no-man's land between the two armies, so as to "redeem slaves." The idea was to buy off, in the South, slaves captured in the North. Controversy immediately arose. The principle seemed wrong for two reasons. First, by buying slaves the trade was being encouraged, since demand was being increased on "the market." The principle that established the non-cooperation with those responsible for the slave trade was thus violated. Second, the slaves so liberated began to grow exponentially, to reach the thousand units for every trip. Eibner collected funds all over the world, but especially from American Blacks, who were particularly sensitive to the issue. Photos of hundreds of slaves waiting in the background, while Eibner negotiated under a tree with a turbaned Arab broker, were seen around the world. I smelled a rat, but the photos were attractive and the news almost a scoop. Furthermore, anti-Islamic prejudice was being fuelled, and in the great circus of the mass media, where everybody is supposed to enter in unison, nobody refused to publish them. Sadly, even the odd churchman fell for it.

It is true that the Arab populations bordering with the South still practice slavery, and even truer that all have the duty to intervene in favour even of a single slave. But the intervention has to be the right one. But the numbers disconcerted me: the yearly crop of slaves could not exceed a few hundreds, whereas Eibner was raving about tens of thousands of slaves, and collecting funds in proportion. I allowed myself to air some doubts in an American magazine, but Eibner threatened to sue both me and the magazine.

In 2002 I suggested to an American journalist to interview Fr Mario Riva, a Comboni who knows the ins and outs of that zone as no one else. Faced with his eyewitness report, even the SPLA, which had protected the fraudsters until then, had to admit that it was a farce. The "slaves" were villagers press-ganged into acting, and the money ended up in the pockets of local potentates, including the mysterious Arab broker. He was no other than an SPLA officer with the skin sufficiently light-coloured to play the part of an "Arab."

No one that I know of ever gave the lie to the issue with the same emphasis as the famous photos. Eibner and his association quietly faded away from the Sudanese horizon.

I have never been able to discover whether Eibner was a victim, or a principal, of the fraud. The sad, bitter fact is that the superficiality of the "great international press" highlights the naivety, or worse, of churchmen who do everything to raise funds, and the ease with which public opinion can be manipulated.

The Resilience of the Poor

Travelling through Nuba land, I saw a primary school with 400 children hidden in the bush. There were no books or writing implements, but it worked. I passed by courts of law operating under a tamarind tree, first-aid centres where traditional remedies were being used together with medicines smuggled in from government-controlled territory, and market places, where on fixed days people meet to barter from hand-made cloth to home-grown cotton to agricultural tools forged from bomb fragments. In the whole of Nuba land there is not a single typewriter or motor vehicle. Electricity, batteries, radios, sugar, coffee and even tea are luxury items. But the Nuba are not willing to surrender.

I wrote the above in 1996. After the ceasefire of January 2002, which was to a great extent respected, the situation has steadily improved.

Religion, not any particular one, but all, had been one of the pillars that has propped this culture of resistance during the long years of war. Christians of all denominations and tolerant Muslims see God as the defender of their rights. Believers can easily come together, for tolerance is part and parcel of Nuba tradition. It is not unusual to find Christians and Muslims in the same family. I was moved one day, when before celebrating Mass in a village, the local imam welcomed me and asked permission to pray with us: "I know the Our Father, and should like to pray it together with my Catholic friends." At the end I asked him to say a word, and he spoke of our common divine filiation.

Today, especially in the West, too many see diversity as a threat. Despite high-sounding words about democracy, tolerance, and cultural exchange, when it comes to the emotional level, otherness is seen as an absolute evil. Widespread anti-Islamic prejudice has never been stronger. Exclusion and self-isolation are becoming the worst social sin. It is not hatred. It is the refusal to consider the existence of the one who is not like us. Fear and rage await the one who does not form part of our narrow circle of friends.

Increasing discrimination can be noticed within the great religions, between those who interpret it in an exclusive mood, fanatic, fundamentalist and generating division, and those who interpret it openly, generously and inclusively. Christian fundamentalists and Muslim fanatics have more in common than they realise.

And yet we Christians believe that all persons are made in the image of God, and God is Trinity, a mystery of relation and love for the Other. How can we propose acceptance, encounter and openness to people who are viscerally incapable of accepting others? Some theologians propose the image of the embrace, to overcome that of exclusion. The following can be proposed as an image worth exporting: two Nuba acquaintances meet along a path. They touch each other's left shoulder (perhaps indicating the heart) with the right hand, followed by a hearty hug. I have seen an image of inter-religious tolerance among the Muslim elders of Kerker. They had all the reasons to harbour hard feelings towards me, since almost all the youth of the village have become Catholics following a catechist who had been instructed by Fr Fenzi, one of my confreres. But when they see me from afar they wait for me with open arms and welcome me in the venerable circle of white-haired heads and white flowing tunics.

In a moonless night I walked for three hours in almost total darkness, in thick bush. We skirted a government garrison, not wanting to be detected. The grass was burned. A faint path was all that could be seen. Earth and sky were dark, with the glittering stars as the only light. My scouting guide looked as if he would be swallowed by darkness any moment. Our whitish path looked as if floating on darkness, suspended in space and time. No sooner we were beyond danger, not too far from our destination, than a catechist began to recite the Rosary. The small group of about twelve, an armed escort and a group of young volunteers accompanying me answered to the repeated Hail Marys, including two Muslim SPLA men.

Re-reading my notes on that first year of travelling on the Nuba Mountains, I find that Jean Hélène, correspondent of *Le Monde*, was with me. He was a first class journalist in love with Africa. He was killed in Abidjan, Ivory Coast, in 2003.

In June 1996 a Sudanese priest and a confrere had come with me for the first time. We arrived at Teberi, near our landing airstrip. A few days later the group split: Jean Hélène left with a guide; Albert Mori, the two Sudanese and I went to pay a visit to some Catholic communities. We covered 200 kilometres in two weeks. On June 29th a great welcome awaited us in Lubi, where for 15 years no priest had been seen. We found that not only the Catholics, but people of every faith received us with open arms. Wherever we stopped, there was an explosion of spontaneous joy, and people brought food and hand-made articles. They saw in us a hope of peace, or at least the possibility of returning to a normal state of affairs with the outside world.

The drama of genocide was staring at us in the face. There was a lack of everything not produced locally; there was no salt, soap, clothes, medicines or school material, just to name what we usually consider "essential." Leprosy and malaria were returning with a vengeance, but there was no medical assistance of any kind. Dozens of people with the first symptoms of leprosy came asking for a cure.

The tension rose with government raids during the dry season. Crops and cattle were looted, what could not be looted was burned, women were raped and people transported to peace camps.

On 30th June I came down with food poisoning, some 50 km from Teberi. Together with Albert and Joseph Aloga I made the effort to return to base, hoping to rest there. But we found that, that very morning the Aggab garrison, some 30 km away, had started shelling towards the Teberi airstrip. The SPLA people asked us to move to the nearby mountain for safety. The heavy military column had left Aggab towards Teberi with the clear intention of capturing us and taking control of the airstrip.

The contingent consisted of about 20 vehicles and 1 000 soldiers. The SPLA ambushed it repeatedly. After three days of fighting, the soldiers holed up in Debi, some thirteen kilometres from the airstrip. From the mountain we could hear the din of battle until the morning of July 5th.

On 3rd July we listened to Radio Omdurman, the official government broadcasting station. It waxed lyrically about the Nuba finally at peace with the government, and praised to the sky the historical bonds and friendship between them and Khartoum. We had to raise the volume to hear all that as the battle was raging.

An aircraft landed at Teberi in the morning of the 6th to take us. We had got off the mountain the evening before. To our consternation, Jean Hélène had not returned. There had been no battle that morning, but as we approached the plane, heavy fire started from the direction of Debi. The first shell missed the aircraft by a dozen metres. The soil lifted by the explosion hit the pilot, who was still unloading. By luck, thanks to the proverbial Sudanese lack of marksmanship and to the reaction by the SPLA, other shots missed their mark by a wide margin, and we took off. We then came to know that Jean Hélène had missed the flight by minutes; it took more than a week for him to be fetched by small aircraft from an improvised airstrip.

In August 1995 I landed at Teberi for the first time. The pilot was Johannes, a Dutchman who for more than a year was the only one who agreed to fly me. We happened to overfly a government position. We could make out not only the vehicles, but also the people who were looking at us. He commented: "First I am convinced that they have no anti-aircraft guns, and second, you will see: they will pretend not to have seen us. Should they report having seen an aircraft, they would be ordered to go and capture it, and they have no gumption to do it." The low morale of government troops was well known. There were exceptions, but generally speaking they were unmotivated and unwilling to fight, except when the enemy suddenly confronted them, and even then, they wanted to flee.

The war properly so called was one of low intensity. Of the two million casualties, 100 000 of which are from the Nuba Mountains, those accounted for by military engagements were very few. There was however, an epic battle lasting two or three months. Malik Agar's soldiers came to rescue the Nuba of the southern Blue Nile. The casualties did not number beyond the hundreds. The main sufferers were the civilians, away from the battlefields. They were kidnapped, murdered in extrajudicial executions, with no medical assistance, no food aid, no possibility of bartering the essentials, and with extremely poor hygienic conditions. Hunger kills more than the sword.

From the purely military point of view, and until 1999, when the government started exploiting the oil, it was a war of the poor. On one side was the SPLA, which counted on weapons and ammunition captured from the enemy; and on the other the government army, badly armed and equipped. Half despairing and half amused, Kuwa told me the following story. His men had bloodlessly captured a military convoy of four Toyota pickups with small artillery pieces mounted on the rear. He went to see them with some other commanders, and what did he find? That the soldiers had shredded the tyres into strips to make *tamut takhali*,[18] indestructible rubber sandals. The vehicles were an instant write-off. They burned them to prevent the government from re-possessing them.

On another occasion, in 1996, the SPLA had lost Teberi, Regifi and Debi. The following year Kuwa led his men to the recapture of the three places. Against Kuwa's orders, some of the commanders, no sooner had they retaken the positions than they went to the stores to see what they could take away. The reaction of the government took them off guard and they had to retreat.

[18] Arabic for "you die and leave them" for someone else to use.

The Southern Blue Nile

As the frequency of my visits to the Nuba Mountains increased, that to South Sudan decreased. And in August 1997 Garang in person denied me permission to go there.

A year earlier, on 17th August 1996, an SPLA commander wanted to lay his hands on two lorries loaded with supplies for the Diocese of Rumbek. He invented an excuse and arrested all the missionaries: the Vicar General Fr Raphael Riel, a Sudanese, three Australian sisters, two of whom were in their 70s, and two Combonis, one a brother and the other a priest. As the one in charge of the Sudan Catholic Information Office (SCIO), I accompanied Msgr Mazzolari to Mapuordit to negotiate their release. They treated us like dogs. We returned to Nairobi with empty hands: the six were still prisoners. To take a consistent line of action we held a meeting at the Italian Embassy, in the presence of the Australian ambassador and a member of the US Embassy in representation of the CIA. I was for publicising the whole affair: the Sisters had been accused of Islamic propaganda, following the finding of a bookmark in their breviaries with a phrase from the Gospel together with one from the Qur'an. The Australian ambassador was for keeping a low profile, since an Australian pilot had been hijacked by the Somalis and was still held in captivity after six months. He insisted on a news blackout so as not to exacerbate the Somalis.

The conclusion was that everyone should act independently. I issued a press release, signed by myself, spelling out the details of the story. Two days later Garang, duly embarrassed, released the missionaries and withdrew the unofficial accusation that they were spies on behalf of foreign countries trying to "spread Islam under the disguise of the Cross." Some Nuba friends remarked, "Garang will never forgive you." Speaking to the Apostolic Administrator of Rumbek, Msgr Mazzolari, I insisted that Garang was to be approached, and a procedure to be followed in like circumstances established. At the end of September that year, Msgr Mazzolari forwarded the proposal to the bishops of the New Sudan (as South Sudan is now known). They agreed, but the delegation was made up of two people: the bishop of Tombura-Yambio and myself. The meeting ended unsuccessfully, with Garang complaining that the Church was hostile to the SPLM. That was the last time I saw him. In July of the next year, a great meeting was held at Yei, a town in Western Equatoria. Representatives of the New Sudan Council of Churches (NSCC) were present in force. The communique said that "the essential role of the churches in fostering a vision of a New Sudan" was acknowledged, as was their right to "contribute to the social and political formation of the Sudan and to be a voice for the forgotten poor." In reality Garang had succeeded in conning them with the usual spiel about Church and State cooperation: the real meaning was that the Church had to serve the SPLM. And the bishops had gone home happy.

I was unable to participate to that meeting, although I had been designated as one of the members of the delegation. I had applied for the entry permit as the one I had was about to expire, but on the day of departure it had not arrived. Was it a bureaucratic delay? The following month I ran the risk and went to Rumbek, which three or four months earlier had been retaken by the SPLA. I was accompanying the last US ambassador to Khartoum. Since then the US and Sudan have broken diplomatic ties. Mazzolari had insisted that I should accompany them despite my lack of entry permit, and alleging that as they knew me there was no need of it. But on descending the stairs together with Andrew Awour who was on his first visit to Sudan, I was turned back. I spent the whole day inside that small plane, from 9am to late afternoon, under armed guard.

From that day southern Sudan was no longer on my schedule, except on the occasion of Yousif Kuwa's funeral. He died of prostate cancer at the Norwich Hospital, near London, on 31st March 2001. His body was flown to Nairobi whence it proceeded to the Nuba Mountains. I had been invited, but the journey necessitated an intermediate landing at Yei. A celebration was to take place there with all the chiefs of the SPLA, apart from Garang, before the burial at Luere. I promised Abdelaziz that I was ready to drop everything to come, but that I was reluctant to end up in jail in Yei, as I still lacked an entry permit. Abdelaziz reassured me. On alighting from the plane, I bumped into Salva Kiir Mayardit, one of the top brass closest to Garang.[19] "Oh! It's you? OK, no problem." He was the one I had had talks with, after the withdrawal of my permit, and who had accused me to have leaked SPLA military secrets, none of which I actually knew.

Shortly after the August 1997 fracas at Rumbek, I had gone to see Kuwa, worried as I was that I did not have an entry permit.

"And now? How do I come to the Nuba Mountains?"

"Don't worry, Father. Continue to come to us, there is no problem."

Other commanders had told me later that Garang and Kuwa had quarrelled over my permit. Kuwa was reported to have said, "Fr Kizito is still without a permit? No matter. He will continue coming to the Nuba Mountains, as everyone knows him there. He needs no permit from the SPLA.

The story is emblematic of Kuwa's vision of human rights and of civil administration. For him these issues were more important than military questions or reasons of State. He was the first SPLA

---

[19] After Garang's death in July 2005, Salva Kiir Mayardit, took over as head of SPLM/A and therefore, President of South Sudan and to join Vice-President of the Republic, under the term of the CPA.

commander to accept an independent monitoring of human rights. An expert like Yohannes Ajawin says:

> Yousif Kuwa is a rare specimen within all the African liberation movements. He always remedied any violation of human rights against civilians, perpetrated no matter by whom: soldier or officer.

One must take into account that Kuwa needed allies: it would have been absurd for him to organise a Nuba movement unhitched to the SPLA: it would have been swept away. Nubaland is "too captive to geography" to advance certain pretences, he used to repeat. He was thus playing a balancing act: on the one hand he pledged absolute fidelity to Garang but in practice his obedience was not all that blind.

Because of the enormous distances and of difficult communication, every SPLA commander had a free hand in his decisions, and at times there were abuses. There were areas where people considered the SPLA as an army of liberation, and in others as an army of occupation.

There is another unusual SPLA leader, in the unusual situation of the southern Blue Nile. The region is in the North, centering on the Ingessena Mountains, but the people are Africans. At the negotiating table, the Nuba Mountains, this region and Abyei tended to form the crux of the talks. Khartoum wanted to consider them a separate issue, according to the principle of divide and rule, but Garang brought the question to the fore at the right moment to raise the stakes. The local SPLA commander was Malik Agar Eyre, friend to Kuwa and Abdelaziz. In February 1999 Kuwa told me: "I would propose to Malik to invite you. Everybody knows that you are not welcome in the eyes of most SPLA commanders, but if he invites you it's a good sign. And I would also repay a big debt I have with him. In 1991, when the Nuba were about to be crushed, Malik came to our rescue with more than 1 000 men and saved the situation. He is now in difficulty and no one talks about the southern Blue Nile. You who have helped the Nuba so much, and Malik knows it, could perhaps do for them what you have done for us. Bring there a troupe of journalists and let them bring the case for the southern Blue Nile to international attention. Are you ready, Fr Kizito?"

My company on the Nuba Mountains, apart from the young men of Koinonia, had always been the Press, with journalists and photographers from many countries. One of them was Maria Grazia Cutuli, later killed in Afghanistan. Her newspaper had not wanted to support her trip, so she took some leave and came at her expense. I had warned her on the telephone that the trip would be a hard one. She assured me: "I'm used to such things. I've been in Bosnia. I've seen worse things, I've no problems." In those days, taking off from Loki meant diving into the unknown. There were no satellite contacts and no sure communication. After crossing the Nile, half an hour from landing, she had a crisis: "I want to go back, I've never been so frightened. We're isolated from the world, from everything. I want to go back!" Luckily another woman journalist succeeded in calming her. She had her own crisis later, completely worn-out by a long walk under the February sun. Finally, when we left Kerker to reach the airstrip for the return flight before dawn, on a moonless night. The two journalists were using their torches to light their path. Musa warned them that the light could give us away. Shortly, a burst of machine-gun fire tore above our heads. We froze and flattened ourselves against the ground, instantly switching off our torches. Our guide Musa shouted a password and heaved a sigh of relief: "They're ours." Then he addressed the patrol: "Why did you shoot?" The soldier who had pulled the trigger explained: "We knew about you, but when we saw you stop at a house, we thought you were the enemy intent on kidnapping someone." We had in fact stopped to say goodbye to a friend Yakub, who was up with all his family. And, for the SPLA torches were a sign of enemy presence, as the SPLA never use them. Musa had warned the two women journalists, too gently perhaps.

Another colourful journalist in our group was Tomo Kriznar, who doubles up as anthropologist. He lives on almost nothing. He starts his journeys with 100 dollars, some tobacco and lives with the people. In 2003 he went alone to research on the Kachipo, who live in Sudan, north of Lokichoggio near the Ethiopian border. He got lost and strayed into Ethiopia. In no time he was in prison in Addis Ababa, accused of terrorism and of complicity with Bin Laden. On getting the news I informed some Nuba, who alerted their acquaintances in Addis. Tomo was released and repatriated directly. But he lost all the photos of the Tochos he had taken during the adventure. The Tocho are of Nuba stock, but unique. No one knows why, when a stranger arrives among them, they welcome him according to the general rules of African hospitality, and give him everything. Everything, that is, except speech. Everything takes place in silence. When the guest leaves, they burn everything he has used. Very few of them joined the SPLA, although one of them was seen holding Kuwa's coffin. There is a Catholic community among the Tocho, as a Tira catechist who succeeded in integrating told me. I have yet to go there.

The Other SPLA

J agreed to Yousif Kuwa's proposal to go and visit the southern Blue Nile. Early in April 1999 I received Malik's invitation and went to meet him in Nairobi on his first visit there.

A group of journalists and I left in November. The SPLA controls at least 150 000km² of territory of the area, but the government defends the environs of Damazin on the Nile with tooth and nail: it is the site of the dam that produces power for the capital city.

At Kurmuk, Malik showed us some prisoners of war (on the Nuba Mountains I never saw prisons). There were 180 of them mostly from the South. Some were Nuba, others refugees from around Khartoum. All claimed to have been press-ganged into government forces.

Some were Arab youths claiming to be 17: they had been there two years. Their conditions were difficult; food was scarce, but all in all it was no harder than for the local people. The prison was the former bank of Kurmuk. By day the prisoners got out under escort, to work and to fetch water. The Southern Sudanese are used, in extreme cases to eating anything and survive; the Arabs less so, and those boys looked run-down. An idea struck me:

"Malik, it would be good for you and your image if you gave me four or five of the prisoners in a bad state for Christmas, at the beginning of the Catholic Jubilee Year 2000: it would be a sign of good will. We take them to Nairobi, nurse them back to health and let them go wherever they want, either Khartoum or elsewhere. We shall duly publicise the affair."

"No problem, Father Kizito. These are really poor people."

Malik was huge: he looked stern, but was really of peaceful disposition. He was scheduled to fly back with us. We could have taken the prisoners.

His problem was the bodyguards, a good portion of his entourage and the secret services, all Dinka. So that next morning he backpedalled: "Let me ask the chief. In Nairobi I will tell you." Once in Kenya I rang him every now and then to have news. For four or five days he promised he would give them to me by Christmas. One day I arrived at Kuwa's office and found him there. Despite his enormous size and a bull's neck, he looked crestfallen. I gave him an enquiring look.

"Garang told me: 'The privilege of releasing prisoners is mine and mine alone. Let me think and I'll tell you.'"

It meant that the authorisation would never arrive. Kuwa, half disconsolate and half indignant, berated him:

"I told you! Don't say anything to him! You are independent and as a commander you must take your own decisions."

It was not a simple difference of character. The great difference between Kuwa and Malik was that the Nuba's geographic isolation was a blessing in disguise. Kuwa was able to send home all the Dinka who at the beginning fought in Nubaland. They were most happy to return home. The fact that the SPLA is under Dinka control made it appear, in those areas where the Dinka are not welcome, as an army of occupation.

The Nuba branch of the SPLA had now become a separate SPLA under Nuba control. All the personnel near to Kuwa, like Ramadan Orandi, who was barely a youth at the time, were Nuba. On the southern Blue Nile things were different. One day, during that same trip, I realised that we were surrounded by spies who knew all about and kept an eye on us. Malik had promised: "Go wherever you wish, tell me what you want to see and I'll give you a car."

This was a luxury. Up to the ceasefire, on the Nuba Mountains one could move only on foot. I replied that we wanted to visit the prisons, and he promised: "At 4pm you will visit them." The prisons were within walking distance. But we found that the soldiers tried to boycott our visit, against Malik's indications. The armed men on guard not only refused to let us in, but also prevented us from getting in touch with Malik, a couple of kilometres away. When Malik came to know he was furious. We visited the prisons the day after, but he had to come in person to acompany us and make sure we could enter the building. Evidently the situation on the Southern Blue Nile is conditioned by its location. It is much easier to reach than the Nuba Mountains, so that for the SPLA top brass it was easier to keep Malik under control. To go to the Nuba Mountains, on the other hand, the Nile stands in the way, as does Bahr el Ghazal. Nuba inaccessibility was tragically demonstrated in 1994-95. Lam Akol had agreed to let more than 1 000 Nuba walk southwards through his territory, with the idea of returning loaded with supplies carried on their heads. There was no other way. On the trip down, by the Nile, a disconcerting number of them died. It was a true hecatomb. The few who made it stayed on and joined the local SPLA.

A 1996 episode shows how Kuwa, though faithful to the SPLA, since unity was the indispensable condition for results, was not dominated by Garang's directives. In Britain, a group of friends of the Nuba had drafted a plan together with Malik, Kuwa and Lam Akol. The idea was to supply the Nuba, who were at an all time low at the time, from Ethiopia. The porters were to leave from Asosa, enter Sudan until Kurmuk and turn west for the Nuba Mountains. They needed to cross the area controlled by Malik, to arrive thereafter to the Nile controlled by Lam Akol. Then they would enter Nuba land. Most probably, the British friends saw it as a humanitarian plan, but the three commanders spotted a way of getting military supplies. Another non-military reason why Lam Akol's cooperation was necessary was that if the Nuba and the Funj on either side of the southern Blue Nile had tried to cross the Nile, they would all have drowned. Akol got the help of the Shilluk, who offered to ferry the supplies from the Funj on one side of the river to the Nuba on the other side. Since Akol and Garang were long time enemies, I asked Kuwa:

"Does Garang agree?"

"Not too much, but he agreed. The operation is top secret, because if the government comes to know, they will send barges along the river and intercept the supplies. For as long as the government is in the dark, the thing can work."

The government was aware of the enmity between Akol and Garang, and could not imagine that they would cooperate in any way. But when everything was ready, the plan was leaked by the *Sudan Democratic Gazette* of Bona Malwal, a Dinka operating from London. The suspicion is that the order to leak the plan came from Garang in person to block the operation when it was about to take place.

Lam Akol, Kuwa and Malik, on the other hand, have always worked on the same wavelength. I thought that there could have been bad blood between them, but I verified personally that it was not so. They did not see things the same way, but respected each other a lot. Akol corroborated this: "Even divided, we stay in touch." He recalled another example of military cooperation: during a battle near Malut we captured a good quantity of ammunition for a German-made firearm that we didn't have, but Yousif's soldiers did. We gave it all to them after taking them from the Khartoum military. Once, while on the phone talking to Akol, I asked him if he knew the whereabouts of Kuwa: "Do you know if he is around, or on some errand for some of his things?" He laughed aloud: "Abuna! He's here, at my home!" Officially they were political enemies, but whenever Yousif travelled to Nairobi he always paid Akol a visit.

The three were the SPLA exponents more attentive to human rights and civil issues. The reason could have been that Kuwa was a teacher, Akol and Malik were university lecturers, whereas Garang, Kiir, Kerubino, Nyuon and the rest of the top brass were military men fighting a war for the sake of power and not of human rights. That's where the problem lies.

The Humane and the Military

There was a firearm galore on the Nuba Mountains before the ceasefire. Every home had at least one, for defence against the government army. Even groups of Kerker children used to go to school armed. Those coming from far, in wartime, moved in groups, and it was not unusual to see the oldest of them, a boy as young as 14, shouldering a Kalashnikov to defend the group.

Despite the widespread presence of firearms, their use was very strictly controlled. At Mogadishu, in 1991, the rattle of machine gun fire could be heard the whole night long; here one could stay for weeks without hearing a single gun report. The merit goes to Kuwa: he kept the use of weapons under severe control, preventing them from becoming a means for extorting food, women or anything else, as had happened in the South. On the Nuba Mountains such abuses happened very rarely, and only at the beginning. They were repressed sternly, even by punishing the culprits according to wartime military penal code. Kuwa set up efficient civil courts of law, forming the magistrates with the help of Sudanese and foreign experts. One of them was Augustine Ibrahim Shamela, who abandoned the military service to become the head of the Nuba judiciary. I repeatedly passed by his home in the Komo Valley, between Kauda and Kerker. On one occasion he had gone to Nairobi for health reasons, and flew with us of the Koinonia group back to Nuba land. On landing at Gidel, he knelt down and kissed the

127

ground, elated to have gone back to his beloved mountains. Three or four months before the ceasefire he was assassinated, seemingly by hired hands from Heiban, which is in government zone.

Abdelaziz found it relatively easy to impose a rigid control of firearms after the signing of the ceasefire at Lucerne, Switzerland in 2002. One of the clauses was that there should be no more arms in civilians' possession; all had to be kept in SPLA armouries. A year later the commander of the Joint Military Commission (JMC) publicly declared, during an NGO conference in Nairobi, that he had seen greater discipline within the SPLA than among government troops. Maintenance was also better: in the SPLA armouries the weapons were kept under control and perfectly oiled; in the government barracks they were neglected. In a garrison they had counted 235 AK47. Next inspection accounted for only 180. No explanation was forthcoming about the missing ones.

My impression is that the ceasefire has held, so far, more because of the mutual goodwill than because of JMC inspections. On the other hand a strict control is extremely difficult in such porous areas. Some control is possible in and out of airstrips, but there are airstrips known exclusively to SPLA people. On the ground vigilance is simply impossible.

Yousif was very keen to have around clean, transparent and reliable people. When he and Abdelaziz travelled to Debi, Yousif paid a visit to the father of a friend. His companions marvelled that he, Commander in Chief and governor of the Nuba, should show concern for an old man who was sick, weak, blind and hardly able to move. But that was the very reason why he wanted to visit him. Abdelaziz reported the dialogue:

"Kurker, I've come to visit you."

"Is it you, Yousif?"

"Yes, I'm your son's friend."

"I'm very happy that you've come. You and John Garang have succeeded in defeating the Arabs and chasing them away from the Nuba Mountains. You may go and call the British now."

Everybody burst out laughing. Yousif, calm, answered:

128

"Why should we call the British? We are going to govern ourselves."

"You're not going to! You can't."

"Why not?"

"You're tribalist, corrupt. You need the British. They were neutral, and treated us equitably. Not that they were good people, but they did not belong here, and had no relatives here. There was no nepotism and no corruption."

Old wise uncle Kurker was not altogether wrong. Some of those present felt insulted: "What? This old man dares say that we are not able to govern ourselves and that we were better off under the British?"

But Kuwa nevertheless treasured the lesson. His first move was to place the administration of justice in civilian hands.

It is now time to get closely acquainted with Yousif, from before the time when he went into hiding. His mother has survived him. His younger brother has this to say of her:

> She taught us to love our land: that's why we grew up with an interest in our country and our people. When Yousif joined the SPLA, she and dad were aware of the step he had taken.

She was at his funeral in Luere, in a beige dress and white foulard, holding a bunch of flowers. Condolences came to her even from people high up in the Sudanese government.

Genesis of a Consciousness

My mother is Zeinab Somi Tutu." It is the opening sentence of Kuwa's autobiography.[20] "My father's is Kuwa Mekki. He used to be a soldier. In colonial days the young Nuba were recruited to fight in the Second World War. My father fought in Ethiopia, actually in Eritrea, in Keren, and fought even at El Alamein. After repatriation, the soldiers were deployed to fight the Nuba rebels on the same mountains. My mother told me that I was born when my father returned from the fight in Tullishi. It was 1945, in the middle of the rainy season. It must have been August.

We were five boys and two girls. Two other siblings died soon after birth. I was born at al-Akhwal, Miri District, where El Akhwal Hill also stands. Whether the hill took the name from the people, also called Akhwal, or vice versa, we don't know. The same happens with Lomon, which is the name of a hill and of the people living around it. It is on the Nuba Mountains.

My parents were Miri. I was the first-born. On the Nuba Mountains we give the name according to the order of birth. A first born boy is called Kuku, a girl Kaka...

---

[20] The following text is an edited version of "Things were no longer the same: the story of Yousif Kuwa Mekki in his own words," in *The Right to be Nuba,* Suleiman Musa Rahhal (ed.), The Red Sea Press, Lawrenceville/Asmara, 2001. With the kind concession of Suleiman Musa Rahhal.

I think Islam arrived during my grandfather's time. Mekki is an Arabic name. I don't know his Nuba name. My father was named Haroun, but on his being recruited changed it for Kuwa. When he returned he gave me the name of Yousif, which is also Arabic. He had intended to call me Mohammed, but since my mother took time to become pregnant, the two of them went on pilgrimage to a *Faki's* tomb asking him to intercede for her to conceive. The holy man's name was Yousif Abu Shara, and that's why my aunt still calls me Abu Shara, Yousif Abu Shara."

Yousif's primary school days registered his first rebellion.

"I think it was in grade Four. The headmaster was a northerner. He constantly repeated, 'Why teach these Nuba boys? They should all go to work as house servants,' and such like phrases. In fact those of us who migrated to the North used to work as house servants. The worst was when the bell rang for the beginning of class. He sat under a tree, while he was supposed to be teaching us. He used to come rarely, and most of the time he would sit under the tree, or do what he wanted, without teaching us. Of course this made us unhappy about him, and the way he used to insult the Nuba people and so on. One day I heard him said, 'Why should I teach these Nuba boys?'

A school rule stated that we had to stand when the teacher entered the room, as we did with our masters the British when they were our colonisers. The next day everybody stood except me, as I could not but remember the insult of the previous day. The headmaster called me: 'Yousif, come here.' I rushed to him. 'Are you sick?' he asked. 'No,' I replied. 'Why didn't you stand up?' I kept silent. He looked at me and told me to go. He did not punish me. That was, as I recall, my first rebellion.

The medium of instruction was of course Arabic. I remember that we were forbidden to speak our native language and were severely punished if we did."

Yousif and his schoolmates began absorbing Arab culture.

"My father was a soldier, posted at Malakal. My school was at Miri Juwa, and I had to sit for my exams at Dilling. But with teachers

131

like the one we had, we could not expect to be promoted to secondary. And so it was. All of us failed. I boarded a lorry from Kadugli to Malakal, where my father was, but on arrival I found that the troops had been redeployed northwards. The soldiers were sent to the South for two years, then to the North, back and forth. These were Anya-nya days. So when I got there he was sent to eastern Sudan, to Jobait, where the headquarters were. I repeated the school year there. I passed the exam and was accepted in Sinkat Intermediate School, which however was not built. I went to Kassala Intermediate for two years, and returned to Sinkat when the school was completed. There I finished my intermediate studies.

Things were going smoothly in those days. At Sinkat we had very good teachers, and we competed favourably with the Kassala school. Our class was the best. Our teachers were proud of us. I was one of the best in mathematics, so much so that when there were difficulties in that subject one of us was called to give a hand to humiliate the other class. Our teacher would berate the Kassala students: 'Look here are the students!' That made us proud.

There were no problems, except that I became aware of being black. It did not seem to be a problem, but our Hadandawa friends used to call any black boy with curly hair *keeshiah*, which means *abid*, slaye. Things changed at the commercial school at Khartoum. Up to then I had been a very good Muslim. I used to go to the mosque all the time. Even during my first year at Khartoum I used to be a good Muslim. But next year something happened that shocked me.

In Sudan, if you are black they call you *abid*, slave. For as long as colleagues and friends do that, one can accept it, but when you hear someone else, especially if educated, use the same word, you feel bitter. One day a teacher was explaining what happens immediately after death.

When you die and they take you to the grave, if you are a Muslim two beautiful white angels appear, they ask you for your name and your religion, and then they open a window for you to go to Paradise. But if you are not a Muslim, a black angel with red eyes, an *abid*, comes to fetch you.

I reacted at once without thinking: 'Even angels, the blacks ones are slaves!' Everyone was shocked. But nobody said anything and the period went on.

In 1964, after the October revolution, women in Sudan were entitled to vote and be elected to Parliament. There was a lot of arguing about it. The Islamic teacher at school asked the students what they thought of it. All expressed their opinions, for and against. I was in favour, since on the Nuba Mountains there is no discrimination between women and men. The teacher was asked to give his opinion. He commented: "Giving women their rights! Women don't work even in their houses: they have the Nuba boys to do the work!"

I could not tolerate that. But after a third incident things began to fall apart. Since the teacher had said things that had upset me, I took to sketching with chalk on the desk. One day I drew an African head. Of course to draw the hair you have to make dots, which made some noise. I was so absorbed in what I was doing as to be utterly unaware of his teaching. All of a sudden I heard: 'Yousif Kuwa, get out of class!' I put my things away and got out. That was the first time in my life to be sent out of a classroom. I felt upset, but later I realised I was in the wrong, and went to the teacher to apologise. But as he saw me he said: 'Go away! You are a very bad student.' I saw that my early protests still rankled for him to react that badly. I had an outburst of rage, kicked the desk and blurted out: 'Why should I stay here then, I should go and work with the Nuba.'

Out of class, I started asking questions. What is this Islam? The only thing I came out with was, that there is God. And I remembered the *kujur* and traditional religion… That episode was a blessing, because to be insulted as a Nuba triggered off my political awareness. Why are the Nuba in Sudan singled out to do the most menial jobs? I began to reflect, more often and deeper each time. Religiously I became a bit of a free-thinker. There came a feeling of disequilibrium, until I read a book that made me aware that we Africans have also our own spirituality.

I called my first-born son Nyerere, because Nyerere is one of the people who really helped me to think as an African.[21] He also helped me from the religious point of view. As a Muslim I used to feel uneasy, as if there is something you are not sure about. Islam taught us many things, but as an African I could see others, like the *kujur*, and the religious practices of my people. Muslims have to reject such things as nonsense. They are *sheitan*, devilish. This created an inner conflict. You are not supposed to believe what you see with your eyes. I didn't feel satisfied: there was no equilibrium between my beliefs and my soul. At the university I read Nyerere's *Let us run while we walk.* The point that really relieved me was this. After independence, people in Tanganyika wanted to discriminate against the British. But he retorted: "The British are our guests, we have to respect them even if they were our colonisers; now they are part and parcel of us." He said that the western media appreciated what he did. But when he opted for socialism the same media said, "Nyerere has turned red," and so on and so forth. Then he said, "Yes, I am a Christian, but I became a Christian at twelve, and I think that we Africans have our spirituality, and I believe in it." And he told a story. Nyerere's father had many wives. One of them had to go to a funeral, and his father sent him with her for a few days. It is part of African tradition that when you leave as a guest you are given a gift.

On departing, the woman's relatives gave her a goat. Young Nyerere was supposed to take it, but the stubborn goat refused to move. One of those present said: "It doesn't want to go? Come." He cut a lock from Julius' head, mixed the hair with some of the goat's, did or said something, and the goat meekly followed Nyerere home. He asked: "Let anyone tell me or explain this religiously or scientifically." And he concluded that we Africans

21 Julius Nyerere (d. 1999), first president of Tanganyika (later Tanzania) fostered African socialism. His thought and experience have been a beacon for all those who dream of a new, proud and free continent, whether Africans or not. And Nyerere had been a teacher, a *mwalimu* like Kuwa before entering politics.

also have our spirituality. That point really relieved me. Up to today I feel I do not any longer have uncertainty about my beliefs. And I decided to call my firstborn Nyerere. Unfortunately he died at two and a half years of age.

In 1964, the Nuba got together and founded the General Union of the Nuba. They began to air their claims. I joined them in 1965. Then I taught for about seven years, after which I pursued a university course, read widely and developed my thinking. I studied political and social sciences at the faculty of economics. In secondary school they had made us read Arab literature, which was not part of our tradition. But at the university I found Chinua Achebe's *Things Fall Apart*. The account opens with a wrestling contest, and since wrestling is part of Nuba culture, I felt the smell of the mountains, from Khartoum where I was. The culture was the same. In Nigeria there is a playground in every village, just as in Nuba land. Late in the afternoon the young men gather there and play, and especially in moonlight. Nobody stays at home. When I finished I felt I had found part of myself in that book. I went on reading African authors. I started to see the differences between being an African and being an Arab, and of course I found myself as an African. Up to secondary school I had felt I was an Arab, because I was taught that! But later I realised how wrong it was. History books, from primary school onwards, had nothing positive about the Nuba. The only thing we knew was that the Turks had come to raid the Nuba Mountains and the South for slaves. That's why the educated Nuba hate themselves for being Nuba. As Muslims they hate their culture, and keep distances from it. They change their names, Kuwa or Tiya or whatever, into Arab ones, and say they were born in Abbassiya, Omdurman or Kosti or anywhere else except in Nuba land. This inferiority complex makes them ashamed of what is called "Nuba."

Up to higher secondary school I was like that. But when the General Union was founded, I told myself: "I've got to be proud of myself." One day, during the Ramadhan fast, which I also observed, I searched for Nuba material in the library. I found Siegfried Nadel's 1947 tome. There I learned my first notions about our rich culture.

It was a strange experience, for up until then I knew nothing about the Nuba, who they were, where they came from... There were other books in that library. And I asked myself: "Why weren't we taught these things in school? It is good history.

I concluded that there was something wrong in Sudan that must be corrected. To begin with, the question of Sudan being an Arab country is the wrong basis on which Sudanism is built. I understood that it was my duty to do something. In 1977, together with other Nuba students, we convoked a seminar for all the Nuba who wanted to change the status quo. The debate lasted four days. We concluded that two things divided our people: religion and tribalism. We understood that if we wanted to change things we had to work from within the system. Most Nuba don't like politics, but we decided first let us unite as Nuba. We began by recruiting the young; it is easy, since they don't usually belong to any party. We founded the Komolo Association. Abdelaziz Adam el-Hilu, Kuku Jagdool and others joined in. We organised a Nuba week with dances of all kinds and even Nuba cuisine. We cooked dishes like *baliela* and *assida*, discussed important events of Nuba history, and compared Nuba with Nubian languages. It was very good. Everything began there.

In 1980 I graduated and went on to teach at Kadugli for one year. It was then that President Nimeiry announced his regional policy, regional government and parliament. Since my degree had a political orientation, there were many things in my mind I thought I could do. But my private life also claimed its rights. I got married in 1980, and marriages are problems. This is what happened.

I was working in the Darfur, to help my parents. A cousin of mine lived in el-Dilling, and I stayed with him every time I returned to Kadugli. One day he asked me why I had not married yet. I said I had no intention of getting married. "It's not possible!" he said, and mobilised all my sisters to put pressure on me to marry. Then he said that he knew two good Miri girls for me to choose. For one year I just sent messages. One day I decided to go and see his offer. I proposed to Fatuma. She did not agree at once, because in our culture women never say "yes." We got married. I taught at

Kadugli for a year, including evening school, and I could pay off the debt I had incurred in marrying."

Kuwa made use of every occasion to stir the awareness of people. Abdelaziz remembers what happened once about music. "One day Yousif brought a tape recorder with East African songs to animate a students' feast at Kadugli. The police burst into the place, confiscated tapes and tape recorder, and they were about to jail Yousif. But he protested: 'I'm sorry, but this music belongs to our African culture.' The police retorted that it went against the behaviour of a good Muslim. Yousif made use of all his dialectic power until he got the tape recorder back. From that moment many young people began to listen to African music as a challenge to power."

Yousif always tried to educate the young to be proud of their Nuba identity without being afraid, and to make use of their Nuba names. Frequently, for instance, Nuba people with high social standing married Arab women, trying to distance themselves from their Nuba identity. Yousif protested against the practice: "It is not racism, but it is an error to marry an Arab woman at this time in history simply because we see that the richest and best educated people are Arabs. Before marrying into their society, let us wait until attaining the same standing. Now all we achieve is to appear as slaves who want to marry their mistresses." He also urged girls not to use skin lightening products, and to be proud of their black skin: "Don't feel inferior, please."

"I liked to teach," Yousif commented. "I had no problems with that. Things changed when the idea of a parliament in the Kordofan began to take shape. I had no intention of contesting a seat. But Ahmed El-Haji, a colleague, said to me: 'You would make the best candidate.' He explained to me how the Nuba were split into two factions: Mahmoud Assieb's and Abd al-Rahman Idris'. They competed so hard that in the end the only ones to benefit from a split vote would be the *Jallaba* of Kadugli, the Arab merchants. And he repeated: "You, who are back from the Darfur and have never entered politics, are the right person to unite the Nuba.' I did entertain political aspirations, but that was not the right moment. I was penniless. 'And which Nuba has money?' Ahmed retorted, unperturbed. 'Ought we to give ourselves into the hands of the *Jallaba* just because we have no money?' We went on discussing, until he convinced me.

I went to the Komolo members. Ahmed was one of them. I explained the situation, asked for opinions, and made it obvious that we had neither funds nor other resources. They replied that we would try with what we had. We plunged into the adventure. I went fundraising in Khartoum, asking for help among university students. Ten pounds here and five there I collected something towards the campaign, but had to cycle a lot to meet people. The *Jallaba* had endless resources, including motorised transport, whereas I had only my bicycle. I used to tell the people I met: 'I have no money. You know that I am only a teacher. My father is not rich either, but I think I can represent you all right.'"

Yousif went from village to village, and people showed appreciation. On one occasion an Arab candidate, son of one of the richest merchants of the area, was holding a rally. He had arrived to the village by car and was speaking through a bullhorn. But people left him and went to hear Yousif, who had just cycled in and was sitting under a tree, panting. After drinking a little *merissa* and resting a little, he started speaking, and struck a chord in the crowd. And he won.

Yousif's campaign was not aggressive. Conscious that his limited means were inversely proportional to his motivation, his style recalled that of fables like the tortoise and the hare, which reward the perseverance and the cleverness of small people.

Yousif spoke: "When the *Jallaba* ask you to join their committee, accept. When they ask you to swear, swear. But if you swear to give your vote to one of them, find ten who vote for me. The *Jallaba* will give you money; take it. Also ask them for one of their vehicles. If they lend it to you, go around in it, even if their symbol is stuck all over it. But do not support them! Thus *Jallaba* lorries took our own people to vote. It was a difficult race. There were ten candidates, eight of whom were Nuba. Every attempt at convincing

138

them to present a single candidate had failed. But the real race was against the two *Jallaba*. My victory was a great shock for them. From that day on the Nuba acquired confidence in themselves. The *Jallaba's* problem was that they believed more in their money than in their ideas. Otherwise they would have realised that things were changing."

Abdelaziz's tells revealing anecdotes about Kuwa. "In principle he had nothing against the Arabs. He used to say, "they're ignorant, they are not formed, they need to know. All we want is to enjoy our rights, after which we can live together." He believed in the unity of the human race, despite the many, hard experiences he had gone through. One day the two of us, in military uniform, were about to reach a Nuba village when everybody started running away. The government had spread the rumour that the SPLA people were thieves coming to destroy and plunder. We bumped into an Arab merchant and captured him. I still remember his name: Abdallah. Kuwa ordered him to his presence. The man was terrified. "Don't be afraid," said Kuwa. And he called some soldiers hailing from Hamra.

"Do you know them?

"Yes, I'm from Hamra too.

"Let me tell you one thing. They have not come to fight the Arabs or anyone else. They're here to fight against the government for having marginalized the Nuba. We're ready to recruit Arabs too. I will entrust you with letters for some Arab notables. I intend to explain to them our message, our mission."

Abdallah relaxed, drank the tea offered to him and even joked. Yousif commented with his men: "Do you see how the Arabs and the Baggara are? They don't believe in words. Until they see with their eyes and experience it, they do not understand. Do you realise our difficulty? But I will not desist; I will lead you until death."

Yousif was always very clear. He unhesitatingly repeated the same message: the problem was not a Nuba-Arab quarrel; the dividing line was between the Nuba and Arabs on one side, and the central government on the other, exploiting and marginalising.

Yousif's brother Musa testified that he spoke to all, confronted all, and respected everyone's ideas. He always gave people a chance. He was not selfish, and wanted to see results for himself as much as for the others. He was not greedy, but above all he was very kind. You could go to ask him anything any moment. He sat down, listened and answered, all very kindly. He was a natural leader. Coming from his younger brother, whom Yousif had looked after with due affection, such assertions may not prove much, until matched with those from all sorts of people that met him. Yousif had in fact paid Musa's school fees, for he wanted to have an educated younger brother. Musa continues: "He himself taught me lots of things, and looked after me until I grew up. I respected him very much. Every now and then we talked politics and current affairs. He was a Muslim, like our parents and all of us, but he explained to me that nobody ought to be discriminated against. 'Certain things belong to God' he used to say, 'and it makes no difference whether you're a Christian or a Muslim. Everyone ought to be treated as a citizen and a brother.' Yousif was not a fundamentalist, for when they imposed the *Sharia'h* all of us opposed it at once."

There are no prominent women struggling for the Nuba cause. But Yousif had feelings for women's status. Musa relates: "He introduced the idea of respect for women among the Nuba, and of their rights. Women's groups were thus born, and they did good work on the Nuba Mountains. It was his idea of citizenship. He didn't want sexual discrimination. He could look into the future. He was a polygamist, and his three wives had given him fourteen children. One day Julie Flint asked him how many wives he had. "Three," he answered, apparently unperturbed. But on telling the story to Abdelaziz, he looked irritated. "Why did she ask me? She knew I have three wives! I know that polygamy is not a positive thing especially from the perspective of women's rights. But the die is cast. I cannot send away my wives!" But he found a witty way out, telling Julie Flint: "If I had to choose again, I would not have married them. I'd have married you!" As in a typical Nuba family, Kuwa's three wives, Fatuma, Hanan and Imm Masar, were at his funeral, next to each other.

Handing Over

J met Abdelaziz Adam al-Hilu, Kuwa's successor at the head of the SPLA-Nuba, long after I had met Kuwa himself. It was early 2001. I had organised a sort of pilgrimage to respond to Pope John Paul II' invitation, on the occasion of the Jubilee year, to go and seek Christ's countenance in the poor. I had announced that the Jubilee would be an African one: to go to the poor of Sudan, and kneel before them. A good number of people responded, some of whom are in touch to this day. But the place had to be kept secret to the last moment for security reasons. But I bitterly repented of the idea, and even got frightened: some of those who had joined it at the beginning, two or three months before leaving withdrew, calling me reckless.

The 27-strong group landed in Nairobi a few days before Christmas 2000. I had met and briefed them on the difficulties of the journey. The programme was to spend Christmas Day on the Nuba Mountains to be back in Kenya by New Year's Eve.

We left for Loki on Saturday 23rd December, hoping to take off on a 748 *Air Services* flight, a local airline that has done sterling service to the humanitarian organisations working in South Sudan and the Nuba Mountains. As the engines were warming up, all of a sudden the pilot switched them off and Kevin, the airline patron, came on board: "A message from Kauda says they are bombing the airstrip. We have to cancel the flight." Then he whispered into my ears: "I'm worried. Since yesterday things have happened that make me think we're being watched. The flight controller has asked me questions he had never asked before about our destination. Yesterday, as we were loading, two suspicious-looking characters were nosing close to the aircraft... This bombing raid confirms that they are waiting for you."

I asked: "And now? What do I do with all these people?" Kevin himself offered to help: "Tomorrow morning I'll fly you back to Nairobi. You tell everybody that the trip is off. On the 26th morning, without telling anyone anything, you come back to Loki with one of our flights. Do not book. You won't have to pay an extra dollar. The aircraft here is already loaded. I will fly you to the Nuba Mountains." And so it happened.

It was a beautiful experience, even though to move around with a sizable group including a number of unfit people was not always easy. We slept at Kauda the first night, and on the morrow we went to Kerker for the rest of the time. Despite our delay, a huge crowd was waiting for us, hailing from all the villages around. In the dead of night Stephen and Ramadan came to see me. "There's a message from Mohamed Juma, Kuwa's second in command. They have intercepted a government radio message. Tomorrow they're coming to bomb. Go therefore to Luere, not Kerker, exactly in the opposite direction. We sat down and reflected. There was something unconvincing. First, it sounded incredible that they had intercepted a government message. Second, bombing never begins before 8 am, in broad daylight. At that time we would already be on the way to Kerker, and when bombs fall the safest place is on the road, where it is easy to hide. Therefore it makes no difference in which direction one goes. Ramadan and Stephen thought it was Juma's expedient. Now Juma was close to a certain ecclesiastical figure who did not look favourably on my presence on the Nuba Mountains. But the Apostolic Administrator of El Obeid was in my favour. That message was an evident trick aimed at ruining our programme. Were we to delay one day more, the people would go back home. It didn't seem right. Ramadan found the solution.

142

At the time Kuwa was in Nairobi for medical reasons, but he was still the one in charge, and we had come with his permission. I wrote to Juma: "Seeing the importance of the initiative and since we have Commander Kuwa's authorisation to go to Kerker, if you give us a contrary order we want it in writing, as a justification for having countermanded his orders."

The written order never arrived. Early in the morning another one of Kuwa's subordinates arrived. He was Mohamed Tutu, a friend who would die in 2002 when his jeep hit a mine. I asked for explanations: "Better left unsaid," he cut short, trying not to embarrass anyone. And he came personally with us and an escort of armed men for protection.

The Jubilee at Kerker was fantastic, with songs, wrestling, dances etc. Lots of people camped in the vicinity of the school, in homes or in the classrooms. Two journalists in the group intended to shoot a documentary about the Nuba, for which they needed an extra week. And there was another attempt at boycotting them. Stephen Amin had agreed to accompany them, but after a few days Juma's men came: "You are under arrest. Your permit has expired and there was nothing written about permission to film. On top of that Stephen Amin, your guide, has not done his military service and has to stay behind." They were placed under house arrest in Amin's house. Luckily they had already filmed what they wanted. Stephen was miffed but not too worried, for he knew the relation between Kuwa and Koinonia. Even the guards were apologetic: "We are sorry... how shall we tell Fr Kizito?" When I was eventually informed, by radio, of what had happened to them, I was able to meet Abdelaziz. There's a silver lining in every cloud.

Kuwa had already explained to Abdelaziz what the trouble was and assured me: "When I'm gone, Abdelaziz will follow my policy. You will have no problem. On the Nuba Mountains Koinonia will continue its activities as before. So, on the occasion of the arrest of the jounalists the message from Nairobi was: "Release them immediately, and get ready to suffer the consequences." When the two cameramen landed in Nairobi, we went together to visit Kuwa.

143

It was the last time I would see him alive. He looked run down: the metastases were everywhere, including the bones, and he was in pain, almost unable to walk. He could have sought treatment earlier, but the attachment to his land made him stay until he could. He was paying the price. He came with Abdelaziz, whom I saw for the first time, and said: "Fr Kizito, I'm very sorry. I don't know how to apologise. It is unthinkable that such a nasty trick should have been played on you. We know who it was, and how many problems he has caused. But on the other hand he has helped with schools, and I don't oppose whoever helps the Nuba. The most serious thing is that he has made use of someone who acts in my name and under my authority. I will recall him here to Nairobi and he will never set foot again on the Nuba Mountains." I replied that we did not want vengeance, and what he had said was enough. But he replied: "It's not only that. He has made many mistakes, including administrative blunders you know nothing about. Next week Mohamed Juma will be here in Nairobi and will never go back to the Nuba Mountains." And so it was. Juma was transferred to the Southern Blue Nile. Kuwa spoke as a patriarch who says farewell to life. "I'm happy that you are here together. Abdelaziz will succeed me. He will know how to manage situations like this."

According to Lam Akol, Abdelaziz is the leader that more resembles Kuwa. "He is an excellent planner, but not that good as a speaker. Yousif, more than a military strategist, was one who thought that the military had to reach targets specified by the politicians, not the other way round. That is why he concentrated more on political issues. His success has been extraordinary, because in no other area has there been such a mature awareness and adhesion to the principles of the Movement by the people. Even the military have benefited from that, considering the isolation of the Nuba Mountains. Had Kuwa lacked such a political vision, he would not have attained such results." Abdelaziz has less charisma than Kuwa ("his shoes are too big for me") but he has shown that he is his worthy heir. Militarily he is better prepared, and politically perhaps more shrewd, while his attitude is rather humble.

144

Three months later we were all on the Nuba Mountains for Yousif's funeral. Stephen and I accompanied the group returning to Nairobi down to the airstrip at Kauda. After takeoff we went back to Luere, on foot as always. About noon the heat was unbearable, and I proposed a short rest under a tree. Within minutes, Abdelaziz passed us with three or four soldiers who greeted us. "I'm getting back my breath," I said. "I too need it," he replied, stating that he had been doing office work and how hard it was getting used to walking like that. After resting we went on, only to find Abdelaziz in turn resting under a bush after a couple of kilometres. He laughed heartily, mostly at himself. Then he confessed: "I've a problem in replacing Kuwa. All knew that he chose me for this post, and people obey me because I am a military chief. But they obeyed Kuwa because he was a natural leader... I will never be able to bridge that gap."

But in reality Abdelaziz too has acquired moral authority as a leader. On that occasion he portrayed well what the handing over meant. The way he acquired his stature of leader was how, immediately after Kuwa's death, he repulsed the military offensive by Khartoum, which hoped to find the Movement demoralised and unmotivated. Perhaps even Kuwa would not have been able to act as efficiently as he did. The year 2001 marked truly terrible moments. The only areas under SPLA control were the plateau of Kujur Shabia, Luere, and rather miraculously, Kerker. Government troops were a couple of kilometres from Kuwa's grave when the SPLA regrouped and counterattacked. The rest of the area, the Komo Valley and the Gidel plains were in government hands.

Abdelaziz's own family history is part of the Nuba efforts to seek safety on their mountains. He was born there in 1954, but his parents hailed from Dar Masalit in the Darfur. He tells the story: "My grandfather was killed by the French, who at the time were pushing for expansion towards East Africa. My family fled eastwards, towards the British. Many were going in the same direction, since the British were setting up Gezira with its cotton plantations. But my father, who was a small trader, stopped here on the Nuba. I have never been in the Darfur. I am from that area by blood, but I have become a Nuba by choice. My struggle is in favour of all the marginalised people. Because of my personal history, in 1991-92 I was chosen as a field commander of the SPLA for the Darfur. We left a message there to the effect that this arrogant government can be defeated also on the battlefield. And today the Darfur has taken up arms to defend their rights."

"I joined the SPLA in November 1985, and shortly afterwards I became Yousif's aide-de-camp. I was given the commission of a battalion in the region of the Blue Nile. As Yousif's second in command, I did my first recruiting on the Nuba Mountains in 1989, and everything developed from there. After the Darfur campaign I became responsible for southern logistics, and in 1995 I headed the New Sudan Brigade in the area of the Red Sea. In 2001 I returned among the Nuba as Secretary of the SPLA. It was my first political appointment.

Immediately afterwards he got his stripes as Kuwa's successor. During the 2001 Khartoum offensive, he gained everybody's respect for his courage in leading his troops at the risk of his life. He is not the type of commander who gives orders from the rear. And some of his men complained: "He runs too much risk, what if we lose him..."

J Believe in Koinonia

The engagement with the liberation movement, my insertion in a society so new for me, the problem of peace to be announced in a war situation, my personal relation with Kuwa and the Nuba, their welcome despite my total ignorance of Arabic and of their local languages, has its prehistory.

Ever since I started working with the magazine *Nigrizia* in the early 1970s, I got interested in basic lines of action like Africanisation. By this I meant promoting Africans towards being protagonists in the Church and in the civil society of their countries. From the ecclesial point of view the problem is linked to inculturation, i.e. how the Gospel can take flesh in African cultures without limiting it to liturgical folklore. During my first missionary journey I took part in a conference organised in Abidjan by the French journal *Présence Africaine*. It was the year 1977. The only white people there were a Frenchman and myself. The idea of an African Council was mooted there, and I have always followed the issue with interest. As luck would have it, an African Synod (a weaker institution than a Council) was proclaimed in 1989 by Pope John Paul II, as *New People* was about to be launched. The Synod took place in 1994.

The second interest was for the Africans to take the reins for running their continent. That's why in 1974-75 I contacted the liberation movements of the Portuguese colonies, the ANC in Zambia and elsewhere, and once in Kenya, the SPLA. My interest in such movements had been triggered by an exchange of ideas with Fr Capra, a Comboni operating in Mozambique. It was 1972-73, a crucial moment for the country and for the Church. Frelimo had conquered the hearts of the Mozambicans. Fr Capra said: "We often say that Africans don't get involved in our initiatives, but look here: when they join Frelimo they are determined, they are ready to fight and to die for their country. What do such movements have that is so special as to awaken a capacity for sacrifice that we are unable to awaken?" My confrere's observation inspired me to get in touch with the movements existing at the time. I found all sorts of things: from men who got involved with enthusiasm, resolve, intelligence and ability, like Kuwa, to those who saw the resistance movement as a career, a path to fame or to riches. But my interest persisted. At the beginning of the 1990s I got in touch with the main Eritrean liberation movement, which had asked me to introduce them to the SPLA. I tried, but without much success.

The third line of action, homogeneous with the above, was the laity. The Church has always neglected their growth. We have always allocated the scarce human and economic resources at our disposal to the formation of the clergy and of nuns. My perception is that there exists an enormous potential of people who feel somehow involved, and that they would want to do more and better. To these, and generally speaking to the Christian people, we give very few opportunities for growth. There are many and understandable reasons for this: the numerical increase of Christians, having to take care of a thousand things, etc. But we always end up privileging the same realities, like the seminaries, and invest very little, financially and in terms of personnel, towards a deep formation of the laity. As a consequence lay people's religious formation remains superficial, generic.

The fourth, discovered in Kenya, is the commitment to peace and reconciliation. The four lines of action converge on Koinonia, a living laboratory of all the dimensions inspired by the Gospel. Koinonia is a community of Christian lay people operating at the service of the greater, surrounding community. They grow together within and without, i.e. in the territory and beyond. Starting from desultorily helping street children, then erecting small structures to help them, we ended up asking ourselves how we could intervene in situations of conflict, either small around ourselves or big like that in South Sudan or the Nuba Mountains.

The essential dimensions are communion (*koinonia* in Greek), communication and service. The headquarters are in Zambia, where Koinonia saw the light in the early 1980s. The Nairobi branch manages all the activities on the Nuba Mountains, besides Nairobi itself. At the moment we are thinking about whether to found a Nuba Koinonia or not. They started young, but now a number are in their 30s, and in Zambia even older. At the beginning we lived together. Now common activities, inspirations and commitments are lived at specific times. To make up for community life strictly so called, we spend four weekends a year in some meeting places outside Nairobi. On Saturday mornings we organise meetings for candidates who undergo a year of formation, and during these retreats we all together decide whether to admit them as full members.

In Nairobi, Koinonia consists of three small communities: Anita's Home, Kivuli plus Koinonia House, next to each other, and Shalom House, where only one person lives. The precondition to be admitted is to be economically independent, i.e. with a job. At times one member or another are asked to work full time at the service of the community, but rarely. We want to avoid ambiguity and the possibility for someone to consider the community as a job provider. Kivuli was born as a refuge for street children, but then expanded as we came to know their mothers and siblings. Various activities were started to involve all these people. The children used to come on Saturdays, and soon more often. We started with a wooden shack, which served as dormitory for 15 of them. Financing from abroad helped form present-day Kivuli. Anita's Home was set up initially for girls, but their care is taken by three real families, each looking after a small group of girls.

It can be seen how my Koinonia experience helped in my excursions to the Nuba Mountains. In southern Kordofan I discovered an exciting church, which had survived ten, twelve, fifteen years of isolation, finding its own answers to evangelisation and how to be present in a situation of conflict amidst poor people. The local church was poor and managed by lay people, since there had been no priests for years. We, in our missionary priestly condition, are convinced that when we are chased away everything collapses. But those Christians, and the catechists, were able to go on and to grow, as Church, in their local reality, and during the years of isolation at that.

The Gospel On the Nuba Mountains

J must confess to feeling uneasy, while travelling on the Nuba Mountains, to see myself constantly surrounded by armed men with automatic weapons. I knew they were there to protect me, but I was embarrassed all the same when, after offering Mass and praying for a community gathered in a stone building, my Mass servers, 15-year old boys, would grab their Kalashnikovs and accompany me to the next destination. When the government garrisons where close to where I was staying, armed men were ·posted watching the whole night to prevent regular troops or militiamen from kidnapping me. In the Sudan, the government exerts radical violence on its own people. It is this basic violence, which denies all human rights, that provokes rebellion. But taking sides with the rebels causes its problems. One evening, waiting at Teberi to be escorted, I visited a dozen SPLA soldiers who had been wounded the day before. I could see the result of violence from close by. I was shaken on seeing their mangled bodies. They had tried to protect me and the rest of the group. I was shocked and could find no words to apologise.

Every time I visited the Nuba Mountains before the ceasefire, my happiness at the extraordinary work done by the Christians was marred by constant signs of violence. But what is the alternative?

Christian tradition offers two considerations: the first is that violence, even when made use of for self-defence, ends up into a hardened habit of further violence; the second is that disinterested love has the great power to transform the violent attitude of a human heart.

The presence of Koinonia, beside one of the conflicting parties, was not "taking sides" and trying to destroy the enemy. It intended to be guided by the principle of the Incarnation: God made flesh for our sake. The Christian community as such is not called upon to get involved in power politics, theoretical social problems, legal debates and academic exercises. Christian identity shines on sharing and identifying with the poor and the oppressed. As a Christian I am not asked to stand by the just and the righteous, but with the sinners, and the pariahs, as one of them. I should not even ask myself: "Are the people with whom I identify myself just and righteous?" That choice is not based on moral judgement. The option depends on the principle that the last ones, the pariahs, have the right, yes the right, to Jesus' presence among them. If they are poor and oppressed, I must be among them, without asking questions. Before preaching and judging people it is important to share their life.

That's why the Khartoum regime can be assured that despite bombings, harassment and violence triggered by its policies, catechists, nuns and priests will continue to stand side by side with all the civilians who suffer in Sudan, whether South or North. Fr Matthias Bizzarro, a 70-year old man with a white flowing beard, had set up home on the devastated plains of Dinkaland. A visiting journalist asked:

"Aren't you afraid to live in a hut, in Spartan conditions, under the constant threat of army raids?"

He looked at the journalist in astonishment and replied:

"And if I don't do that now that I'm young, when do you think I will be able to do it?"

Fr Matthias died a few years later.

Not even such missionaries were able to go to the counties controlled by the SPLA. Yet the Catholics, despite being left to themselves, have increased their number. 15 years ago on the Nuba Mountains they were a handful; now they are several thousands. As a rough estimate, 25% out of a population of 400 to 450 000 were Christians before the repatriation after the ceasefire. The Catholics were 8-10% of the 25%, or about 30 000. Three married deacons and the catechists have worked miracles. Returning from my first Nuba Christmas in 1996, I wrote that I had received a rousing welcome from all, Christians and non-Christians alike. All saw that the Christmas celebration was an anticipation of the long-awaited peace, a sign that normal life is still possible. Together with song and dance they brought children for me to baptise, they brought the first fruits of the harvest, they decked me out with bead necklaces, straw hats and bamboo walking sticks. A few hours before leaving a 17-year old boy, with a shy smile but powerfully built, took me aside and put a bead bracelet around my wrist. *"Abuna,"* he said, "Promise me you'll return before this bracelet breaks up. Your presence makes us truly feel members of the Church."

On the same occasion we stopped at Kerker, where the local community welcomed me in a chapel with stone walls and thatched roof. The welcoming ceremony was very warm and intensely felt. The heat in the sun was unbearable, but outside the chapel stood an enormous tree, under which I sheltered. Young people and even some elderly women were performing lively dances. Many were not Catholics. The throng grew by the minute. One hour before sunset the time arrived for the wrestling match, to show their talents in a martial art at least 3 000 years old.

The countenance of those next to me changed. From serious they became ferocious. Their only attire was a pair of shorts. Their bodies were covered in white ashes and yellow dust. As they were taking position, the catechist stood up and said: "Friends, let's not forget that this is sacred ground. Let us move further." My camera was ready, and I did not see any reason for a clash between a local tradition and Christianity. I was tempted to intervene, but I followed the athletes in the new venue. It was one of the most enthralling wrestling matches I have ever watched. With full self-control, even when the effort was at its peak, the wrestlers did not break a single rule of the sport. There were no injuries: whenever there was reason to fear violence, the referee intervened. In the end the two shook hands and laughed together. The loser is the one that first touches the ground with his back. The winner gets no awards other than the satisfaction of winning and the spectators' cheers, songs and dances celebrating their favourite's victory. Before the match, the women removed the bead necklaces from their men, lest they broke. At the end there was a general jubilation with a dance involving winners, losers and spectators.

Later we dined with the elders. The meal consisted of *kisra*, a local type of non-leavened bread made of sorghum flour, pumpkin sauce, onions with peanut butter and goat meat. As everybody was dipping his *kisra* in the sauce, I asked the catechist why he had forbidden the wrestlers to fight in the church courtyard. He explained: "Last year during the dry season a government commando surprised us. They usually do it to frighten and intimidate us by destroying the harvested grain in the stores so as to force us to move to the towns out of hunger and there be controlled by the government. They also do it to punish Christians. The commando found Gabriel, the catechist my predecessor, here in this church, teaching some catechumens. Most of them managed to escape, but Gabriel, who was trying to cover their flight, was captured. They asked him: "Are you Christian?" "Yes," he replied, fully well knowing the consequences. They tried to bind him hands and feet, after which they intended to lock him in the church and set it on fire to burn him alive. It's what they usually do. But Gabriel was a fighter, big and strong, and the soldiers could not tie his hands. One of them, fearing that he might escape, drew a knife and slit his throat. Then they ran away, leaving Gabriel's body on the ground, just outside the church door. That's why we Catholics consider this ground sacred. Here Gabriel shed his blood for Christ."

I was speechless. It sounded like a story from a martyrologium, and yet he was telling it matter-of-factly, as an everyday event. My objections to his order to move the wrestling ground elsewhere evaporated, and my respect for him increased. For this people the choice of Christ is unto death. Their wrestling is not just a sport: it is a sign that they are ready to fight to defend their dignity and their creed.

The three "deacons" mentioned earlier were the three key figures of evangelisation during the war years. In 1995 the Apostolic Administrator Msgr Menegazzo, before his episcopal ordination, came to Nairobi. He gave me a list of eight or nine catechists. No news about them had filtered for a long time. He urged me to check on them, especially the first three. Where they still alive? Had some become Muslims?

We landed in the morning on the improvised Teberi airstrip. In the afternoon Jibril Tutu Jiran, one of the three deacons, came to meet us wearing a surplice, with the stole across from shoulder to hip as if in a liturgical celebration. With him was the older Paul Chalu, who had walked two days to get there from Kerker. Musa Arat, a former Protestant teacher in his late 60s, had not managed to come. The three had not become Muslims. Jibril alone had opened more than 30 chapels in his zone, and had baptised ten thousand adults. A large group of catechists had come into being around him. Before leaving Teberi I promised I would come back in December for a whole month, to hold a course for catechists.

All addressed the three with the title of deacon, even though their ordination as deacons does not appear in any church registry. Possibly they were entrusted with special responsibilities like keeping and distributing the Eucharist, and to supervise the other catechists in their area, and the faithful called the deacons just as a sign of special respect.

In December I met 80 catechists, who had already received their first formation from the three deacons. They acknowledged their having been taught by either Chalu, or Arat or Jibril, in whose zone we were. He was present at the whole course, always at the rear of the class. I spoke in English, and the Protestant pastor translated into Arabic or at times into two or three local languages.

We celebrated Christmas: many who had become Catholic during the war had never attended Mass. Between 5 000 and 7 000 adults converged to the place from all over to take part in the celebration of the Eucharist. They camped all around. For three days more and more people arrived, reaching a total of some 10 to 15 000 on Christmas Day. They had all been formed by Jibril Tutu. It was a very moving scene. Jibril was like the country parish priest of old: when I accompanied him from village to village I could see that he knew everybody; he had baptised all of them, knew their names, their families and every personal story. He was the true leader of the Christian community. One evening we were walking together along a path in a valley not far from Teberi. It was a narrow, long valley, rather bucolic-looking. All, sweating and half naked, were engaged in irrigating their small vegetable patches, neatly terraced, fetching water from the wells with split calabashes. Suddenly Jibril, climbing from the bottom of the valley, intoned a song. All answered, along a good kilometre and a half. People began to bring samples of their harvest as a present to me. A young man, newly married, a regular frequenter of the community, brough a bunch of onions. Joseph Aloga, my first intepreter before Stephen and until the Nuba began to have a smattering of English, urged me to eat, to show appreciation of the gifts. That evening I must have eaten a kilo of raw onions!

Joseph's story is very much like that of many catechists. They became Catholics at Khartoum, or at Port Sudan. He was from Um Derdu, a village some two hours from Kerker. In 1980 he migrated to Khartoum, where he met the Combonis, became a catechumen and was baptised. Then he moved to Port Sudan, where he exercised as a catechist with Fr Peter Coronella. He returned home in 1984 and married. "In the village I found Jimmu Teima" he recalls. "He was a childhood friend who had become a catechist like me. Both of us were enthusiastic with our newly discovered faith." They were not discouraged by obstacles placed in their way by the Muslims. "In a short time a small community began to grow, and we built a church. Meanwhile my wife had delivered our first child and I thought I had settled. It was not to be. In 1985 the Sudanese army arrived and started torching churches. They also came to Um Derdu and torched the chapel. They killed Jimmu on the spot for resisting. Three more Christians were taken away and murdered."

Aloga escaped only because he was away with his wife visiting some relatives of hers in another village. "My only choice was to run away with the whole family. I joined the SPLA as a radio operator, but I gave a hand to whichever Christian community I happened to be with. Today I have two children, and would very much like to see them grow in peace. But there will be no peace for as long as we are treated like slaves." The strange thing is that whenever I asked him to tell me stories of Christians, he invariably answered, "Nothing to report. Everything is normal." That's what he meant by "normal." Had I not insisted with my questions, I would never have come to know his story and others he told me.

I went to Debi, at the base of Mount Lomon, often between 1995 and 1996. The head catechist was Noah, 30, with a large group of Christians who were wrestlers. In July-August 1996 they were all killed during a government offensive that took Debi, Teberi and Regifi.

Some of the 80 catechists of the Teberi course told me other stories. I asked them what had brought them to their faith in Christ, since 35 of them were formerly Muslims. The answers were all alike: it was the example of the three elderly catechists, or of Christians in any case. Angelo, about 20, told the following story: "One day I went to visit some relatives at Kadugli, running the risk of crossing the dividing line between the SPLA forces and those of the government during the night. Next morning I was in Kadugli, a town of some 20-25 000 inhabitants. I was a Muslim, but Nuba-style: Islam among us is watered down with traditional practices. For instance I was 17 and still uncircumcised. At Kadugli I was unfortunately stopped by a patrol:

"You are not a local, we've never seen you. You are a rebel."

"No, I'm not!"

"Are you Muslim?"

"Of course I am."

"Show us that you're circumcised."

They pulled down my trousers.

"You are uncircumcised! You're not a Muslim. You've lied to us. You are one of the rebels. To prison!"

They put me in prison without trial and with nothing beyond what I had on. In prison, whether at Kadugli or elsewhere, you don't eat unless your relatives bring you food, and my relatives didn't know I was there. After a couple of days some other prisoners came to me.

"We've heard that you're a Christian. Would you like to eat with us? We have enough for you too."

"But I'm not a Christian!"

"You say that because you're afraid, but not to worry. Eat with us."

"If you wish I'll eat with you, but I'm not a Christian."

They went on sharing their food with me. I was very impressed at seeing how they helped each other and me too, without belonging to their group... and only because they were Christians. After a while they confided that they were organising a jailbreak. They wanted to break at night; they had bribed some guards who had agreed to pretend they were asleep. We escaped. They wanted me to follow them, still believing that I was a Christian. They constantly referred to this Jibril Tutu. So I too went to see Jibril, became a catechumen and here I am, a Christian."

The gist of the various accounts is always the same. Another Nuba catechist relates: "I was at Khartoum, but had decided to return home because life in Khartoum was unbearable. Speaking to some Nuba friends I told them I was thinking of joining the SPLA, because I knew that in the area controlled by the government we couldn't live. One of them gave me a letter: 'Be careful, it is addressed to Jibril Tutu.' I didn't know who Tutu was, but I still took the risk. During the journey to Kadugli I was searched three or four times, and every time they ordered us off the bus. Shortly before entering Kadugli they ordered us to put our bags down on the ground and stay away. The soldiers thoroughly searched every bag. One of them pulled out the letter, looked at it and put it back. Then he asked: 'Do you know Jibril Tutu?' I tried to defend myself. 'I only have a letter for him… it's not my fault!' 'Don't worry,' said the soldier. 'Tutu is my friend! Deliver the letter and give him my regards.' A little later there was a new inspection, by another group of soldiers: the one who had spoken to me now risked being punished for having let that letter through. But they didn't find it. All that was happening impressed me deeply. I said to myself: 'I'm going to deliver the letter personally. I want to meet this man for whom even a soldier is ready to risk his life.' And so I too became a Christian."

In such communities, recently formed and full of enthusiasm, there was from the beginning a strong demand for doctrine and sacraments, which we have not been able to satisfy. When I arrived, for instance, nobody could explain what the Immaculate Conception was, for nobody had ever heard of it. But the essential was there: the acceptation of Christ and of the Church. On that basis anything can be built: the doctrine proposed in the catechesis is immediately received and interiorised. The communities, however, were trying to respond somehow to the need for the sacraments. The rumour was abroad in areas under government control, and therefore where the dioceses worked, that there were catechists acting as priests. I discreetly inquired, but did not find anything sure. In my opinion they were holding ceremonies, but without any pretence of their being Masses. In fact ever since my arrival these celebrations had stopped, which made me think it was not a consolidated praxis. It would have been very difficult to stop them, had that been the case. Also, the three deacons had an extremely strong ecclesial sense: they had instilled in the people a community spirit and obedience to the bishop. Two of them told me: "Pre-adolescent girls go to harvest *durra*. This is stone-ground, and the flour is used to prepare *kisra*. The elders and all of us get together and pray over the *kisra*, asking God to turn it into a sign of His love and presence among us. The *kisra* is then distributed and consumed during prayer time. We know very well, as do the faithful, that this is not the Eucharist; but it helps us to push on for as long as we don't have a priest who can nourish us with the Body of Christ." The *kisra* has all the looks of a big host.

I have often reflected on this issue, which ought to be studied under the historical, disciplinary and theological points of view. While sharing my life and celebrating the Eucharist with the community on the Nuba Mountains I asked myself several questions: why, when owing to circumstances out of control for the Church the laity takes over, lay people show such initiative, energy and commitment that one rarely sees in more structured communities? Is it right, or appropriate, to leave communities for long periods, even years, without the Sacraments, particularly the Eucharist? Are the words of Christ "do this in remembrance of me" an order?

The situation is very much like that of the early Church soon after the persecution by Diocletian.

Modern evangelisation began among the Nuba with the Evangelical church, which arrived at the beginning of the 20th century, some 50 years before the Catholic Church. They settled among the Tabanya-Korongo, whose valley became a centre of culture and Biblical evangelisation. They printed religious texts in the local language, for neither Arabic nor English were known there at the time. They even built an airstrip, and at the beginning of the 1980s they had a good group of Nuba Protestant pastors.

The Comboni set themselves up at Kadugli and Dilling in 1954. Fr John Vantini recounts that Charles Muratori, a missionary who was also a linguist-cum-ethnologist, after spending 25 years in the Bahr-el-Jebel felt "an exile" in Khartoum, where his superiors had transferred him. In 1951 Fr Muratori found seven Nuba boys to whom he offered a place in the school and boarding facilities. The seven taught their language, Tira, to Fr Charles. They got interested in the Gospel and were baptised on 8th December 1952. Muratori drafted a small catechism and prayer book in Tira. This was the beginning of Catholic penetration among the Nuba. More books followed, in their languages. Six of the seven went ahead with their studies; one became an MP in the Khartoum parliament, and another became a teacher. The head of the group today sells sweets and biscuits at the entrance of the Comboni College.

Comboni presence at Kadugli and Dilling remained weak, since the missionaries were few. Meanwhile a good number of Nuba boys, going to Khartoum for work, would return as baptised Catholics. Joseph Aloga was one of them. Some became catechists, destined to keep the Church alive for the years without priests.

Beginning in 1974 the Kadugli missionaries began to collaborate with the Tabanya Protestant church. A strong movement of evangelisation began with ex-Evangelical volunteers now catechists of the Catholic organisation. At the beginning there was some resentment; ecumenical dialogue began later and today it is flourishing. Many baptised youths declared their availability for advanced Biblical courses and for the social services organised by the missionaries yearly around the Catholic church of Kadugli. There was also a dispensary for tropical diseases doubling as leprosarium, and run by missionary personnel.

Around Tabanya there arose new communities, in what for decades was a world just touched by the news of the existence of a church in Tabanya, but without knowing its message. The Catholic Church expanded its evangelisation in the Southern Kordofan, but eventually concentrated her efforts on Tabanya and lost touch with the periphery. In 1974 some Moro villages became Catholic through catechists ex-Evangelical. In Tabule, a village of some 800 inhabitants, and Farandalla, next door, Yohana el-Kom, a clever catechist, set up a community with social and religious activities, with a self-supporting church and assistance for the poor. There was a cooperative managing a mill and a dispensary; they even had a school for adults and a kindergarten. They are open to all, without religious or social discrimination.

In 1977 new Catholic communities arose around the area, where Islam commanded 10% of adepts and the rest belonged to traditional religions. In the sizable village of Ngolo the son of the chief converted, took the name Daniel and began catechising and promoting social services. His action extended to the villages nearby, Toro and El Azrak. In 1978 at Demodrigo, in the valley behind Tabanya, Yohanna Akomande, a young man baptised at Khartoum and formed at Kadugli, began a successful small church.

Also at Toroji, formerly linked to the church at Tabanya, a young catechist set up a small Catholic community towards the end of 1984. He was fully backed by the village head, a Muslim, who for this reason incurred the deep dislike of the Arab merchants. The village is strategically important, both economically and politically, for being located on the road from Talodi to Ngolo-Tabanya and Buram. From here, close to the mountains, a road begins. In less than 20km it reaches South Sudan territory. Pariang is the first Dinka village. Everyone there is affable and warm (and Christian too). The road proceeds to Bentiu, further South East, in Nuer land.

Fr Fenzi continues:[22]

At Kadugli the Catholic Church opened and ran new centres of catechesis and social services. There were 47 in 1984. Entire villages had turned Christian under the leadership of catechists who administered sacraments and built churches with brick and mortar. The Blessed Sacrament was kept permanently at Karga (Heiban), Allubu, Regifi and Teberi.

The government itself had unwittingly given a hand to the growth of the Church as well as to the general interest towards the Movement. In 1983, shortly after the SPLA-induced war broke out in the South, Khartoum unleashed a violent persecution, singling out the Tabanya Christians accused of supporting the rebels. The pastor was beaten up and thrown into prison. The mission was half destroyed. He was liberated thanks to the intervention of Fr Fenzi, who reminisces:

The pastor of Tabanya was a local young man, often opposed by his own faithful for his rigorism. The authorities opposed him for having set up communities of staunch Christians. By striking him, they hoped to disperse his flock. The objective was to establish an Islamic centre, thus changing the Christian identity of the Tabanya-Korongo. The resistance of the local Christians and their pastor was sorely tried first by intimidating actions, and then by a true persecution that began in 1986. The same policy was applied to all Nuba Christian communities,

22 Personal communication, May 2004.

whether Catholic or Protestant, at the border with the South, where rebellion was rife.

From 1987 onwards the persecution spread systematically throughout the Nuba Mountains. They were the object of raids not only by the Khartoum army, but more tragically by the Islamic militias; many churches were burned, dozens of catechists and pastors slain, the more educated Nuba disappeared, and thousands of people fled, hungry, destitute and unsafe. The 1985 famine had found the Catholic Church in Kadugli ready. Not only the Catholic communities, but also Tabanya and its pastor, were helped with grain and food. The crucial event was the unjust arrest of that pastor at Kadugli. The charges, invented by converts to Islam paid by Arab marchants, were always the same: collaboration with the rebels or instigation of the people against the government, and contempt of Islam. The object was to slander those responsible for the Christian communities and eliminate them. There were no defence lawyers; a condemnatory sentence was certain, but at times some of the accused died in prison in mysterious circumstances. Malaria, the police used to say. The Nuba who disappeared in such fashion were hundreds if not thousands. Honest Muslims who did not feel like ·supporting the government met the same end.

The pastor of Tabanya was about to go the same way, under the charge of meddling in politics. It was necessary to hurry, above all to give maximum publicity to his imprisonment, so as to discourage a possible silent and swift execution. Even yours truly – Fr Fenzi continues – was denounced by the new governor for "illegal activities" and with the purpose of "safeguarding Islam." He was also arrested but released on bail. The Catholic Church at Kadugli joined forces with the pastor of Tabanya, in prison for months. The Catholic community took the issue to heart, taxed itself to raise a huge ransom and hosted the released pastor until he recovered enough strength to look after his community.

The Nuba understood that the Movement, which they had hardly heard of, must have been good simply because it opposed the government. And the credibility of the Christian message was reinforced all round.

Tabanya is the westernmost part of the Nuba Mountains I have visited. I landed there in 1999, and celebrated Mass in a little church set among the rocks like an eagle's nest. It is a vantage point for the whole plains below. A second celebration took place before hundreds of people. There were Christians of all denominations and non-Christians, crowding the place under enormous mango trees that scarcely let any sunlight through. Some young children fled at my sight: they had never seen a white man... We skirted a government garrison near Buram a few kilometres away. The catechists led me to the ruins of a Protestant mission, which operated in the area between 1924 and 1983. There has been no school in the whole area ever since. They recalled Fr Fenzi very well.

Among the elderly there were some who still remembered Fr Gottardi with veneration. "He loved us! Fr Silvano loved us!" they went on repeating, almost tenderly. Such expressions of affection are a typical Nuba trait. In this they are very different from many other African peoples. Frequently I chance to meet, along a rocky path, an old man whose countenance lights up on seeing me and calling me by name, and an old woman who stops and caresses me. Fr Francis Cazzaniga, ex-Apostolic Administrator of El Obeid and still working as a missionary in the Sudan, has left behind his mementoes. An old man, a Catholic, pointed out to me the valley floor from the top of the mountain we standing. "Do you see those big trees on the edges of the sorghum field? There used to be a small church there, and Fr Francis used to come from Kadugli to visit us regularly. The community grew quickly, because Fr Francis knew how to make us taste the Gospel. He respected us and our traditions. But after the Movement began operating, the army thought they saw rebels everywhere. We had no idea what they were talking about. There was a most brutal repression, especially after the expulsion of the missionaries. The chapel was burned down, and the blackened walls were demolished. No trace remains today. But we resist here on the mountains. When you see Fr Francis, tell him we've kept the faith."

The Protestants too developed a robust local leadership. Many of their pastors ended up in SPLA-controlled areas. The Catholics had no official representative, except the three deacons, from 1983 until my first visit.

In such a situation, the temptation exists of going beyond teaching, explaining, instructing, catechising, by imposing structures and hierarchies. During their isolation, the Nuba church had struck local roots. I always noticed how their constant reference was to the Gospel. It looked as if they followed Jesus alive walking ahead of them. Their growth had also been enhanced from confronting the Muslim community, because the Christians had been forced to understand themselves better, to single out their specificity, and to discover the true countenance of Jesus. I noticed this when talking with the catechists about spiritual topics. They helped me to see the face of Jesus better. My presentation of Jesus Christ was not as forceful as theirs. They had understood – and put into practice – that if we are really ready to meet others, those whom we meet can help us to change and deepen our individual and social conscience, grasping what it means to be together around the Master.

Their conversion to Christ, mostly during the years of tribulation, had a difficult and laborious beginning. Then it became a true path of liberation. It was not taken for granted. The communities founded by the catechists were fully opened to everyone, and their ability to live was tangled with daily problems. The Gospel was a practical guide of how to manage without salt and soap, to meet a Muslim neighbour, to organise wrestling matches and above all to resist the temptation, always present wherever there were SPLA soldiers, to commit abuses.

In the midst of all this there arrived priests who felt they had to impose order. They named the heads of the community instead of letting them be elected, and resumed control of the administration of the sacraments.

Thus did the Nuba church return to the Roman tradition. It had started as a laboratory of freedom and love for the Gospel. Lay people managed church affairs, while all the time keeping a heroic fidelity to the hierarchy, and accepting its restoration however hard. The Nuba church, fertilized by martyrdom, grew as an authentic African, Catholic, church.

Christology of the Mango

J was in Amdrafi for Easter 1997. There I held my last mass baptism, after which I restricted myself to small groups and finally handed over to the newcomers. The Easter Vigil was celebrated at midnight. In torchlight around the Easter fire and amidst the abundant water poured on the heads of the baptised, I preached Jesus' death and resurrection to a crowd of some 140 people, children as well as adults. It was a most beautiful celebration.

Paul Chalu was one of the "deacons" responsible for the evangelisation of the area. At 55, he looked 20 years older. I could see him in action: he always had six or seven youths around him, and he transmitted to them the faith without much need for question-and-answer methods. One day at Kujur Shabia I understood what "discipleship" meant, and what had allowed Jibril Tutu, Musa Arat and Paul Chalu to keep the faith and make the Nuba church grow during the long years of isolation. I saw Paul coming from afar, together with three young catechists formed by himself. He dialogued with them, and they at times entered into an argument with him, although always with the measure of affection always directed at the African elders. The four sat on a rock. It was sunset. Sipping cold water from their calabashes, they were talking about the life of a Christian community. I could see a scene straight out of the Gospel. The Nuba catechists, without formation other than the Gospel, had instinctively followed the method of Jesus and the Apostles in forming disciples. Like Jesus, they announced the Good News and gathered around themselves the more open young men. They walked together, in communion of life, teaching and leading the community together. They practiced discipleship, the method with which the "master" shares the disciples' life, instructs them and exhorts them on the way towards seeking the Kingdom. Together they solve the problems of the growing community. They do not forget that the Master is one, and that they are His weak image, disciples and masters at once. Jesus did not give priority to statistics, but to keeping the tension towards the Kingdom of God, and to give the disciples a sense of life as a journey towards God's mystery. He started by conquering hearts. The fishermen, the Samaritan woman, the tax collector, the rich man, were intrigued by that strange Master, and followed Him. It was love at first sight. They fall in love and let their heart open to the truth coming from the Other. Only then does Jesus instruct them. The Gospel shows us that drawing close to Jesus is not the result of rational inquiry, but of an experience of love. Teaching comes later, little by little, after having said "yes" to love.

In a little Nuba church, with walls of dry stones and thatched roof, the inside whitewashed with yellow mud, I noticed a charcoal-drawn outline of a mango next to a war scene. I asked what it meant. They answered that the juicy, sweet and nourishing mango represents the heart of Christ, also because of its shape.

The conversation went deep into the night. By an almost magic moonlight, Paul and the young Nuba were telling me the story of their community. We spoke of how to give back hope to a girl raped while in prison, and how to nourish the faith of a small group of Christians six walking days away from the nearest community. We slept in the open, on mats provided by the local community. In the morning, after a breakfast of honey-sweetened *durra* gruel, I was staring at their silhouettes melting into the surrounding rocks. Were they four or five? Among them was the Master, for sure.

Africa has been bombarded by all sorts of proposals: political, religious, cultural, commercial, etc., which act there as in the rest of the world. The Christian proposal seems absent, but there is no reason for such absence. That proposal ought to leave the people not only as free as possible, but also open to creativity. The values of the Gospel are service, love of neighbour, fraternity, and the Incarnation. The latter is fundamental, and the traditional religions lack it: God made man, made flesh. By announcing that there is something divine in every person, all the rest will grow organically and naturally from it.

Nuba Homeland and Culture

We Nuba are rooted to our land, like that tree… do you see it? Its roots are deep. You can't take it away. That's how we are." Sodi, the Nuba uttering those words, had the opportunity of following NRRDO courses in Nairobi, but was always impatient to return to his homeland.

It is still difficult to define clearly what the culture of a given people is. It is like its soul, and I will not attempt to define it here. The Nuba have a series of cultural expressions that stand out to the observer, and that let some traits of their soul appear in their beauty, despite years of oppression and denial. The Sudan war was in fact a cultural clash, as Yousif Kuwa used to remark. Relating his personal experience he used to say:

> I've lived more than 30 years in the "old" Sudan. I could not, even for a day, feel at ease with the clash between what I thought and what I had to live with. I think that the sense of life is to go back to be what you really are. For me to be a Nuba means to go back to my roots, to live like my parents, grandparents, ancestors, and finally to attain a balance between what I believe and my lifestyle.

Beauty and aesthetic sense are perhaps the things that strike the visitor to Nuba land first. The beauty of the habitat, with those rocks of the weirdest shapes, rounded or flat like sheer rock faces laid by a giant's hand, serve as backdrop for the harmonious setting of people's houses. On one occasion I could contemplate a small hillock covered with many houses of dry stone, with terracing, pathways and flowers. A baobab crowned the top. I had never seen anything as enchanting in Africa. When children pose before the telecameras, they do so with absolute naturalness, fearless and without crowding around the telelens. There is also a gorgeous body art, and the elegance of Nuba wrestling.

When Kuwa founded the Komolo Association, his main aim was the cultural renaissance of the Nuba.

> The Nuba, oppressed for so long by a forced Arabisation, were ashamed of even being Nuba. Many were shy, without self-esteem. We tried to revitalise Nuba sentiments. We are Nuba, and live as Nuba.

The attempt was not an "archaeological digging," but an opeartion aimed at acquiring values for the present and for the future. If, for instance, the ancient wrestling had elements of danger, like the use of bracelets that could wound the opponent, Kuwa pleaded for their elimination from the sport. He was fully aware of how much wrestling was felt by the people. He recalled:

> Among other things, wrestling is the occasion for a young man to show his strength, his muscles, and his manliness. Women see him in action... and maybe one of them falls in love with him!

He also realised how the war, with its sufferings, hunger and deprivations, had inflicted wounds on the Nuba physique and modified it:

> It's no longer what it used to be! The Nuba were famous for their solidity and their well-built bodies; they were almost giants. Now they are thin and sickly.

How central wrestling is for the Nuba is shown by this experience lived by Julie Flint. She watched a wrestling match at Korongo. But this time the challenge was not so much between two champions as between the wrestlers and the government garrison camped within sight of them. Julie was very impressed. It was as if both the wrestlers and the public were saying, "You want to uproot us, to Arabise us, snatch us from our culture... and look, we are here, wrestling as we always have, living our lives, here before you." It

170

was a real challenge by the Nuba to the government: they wanted to be themselves.

The most extraordinary thing, though, was the fact that the garrison, which could have attacked and dispersed the demonstration, stayed put. The soldiers, three quarters of whom were themselves Nuba, since they were press-ganged into fighting their own people, vibrated at the spectacle, for it was part and parcel of themselves.

Besides wrestling there is another symbol of the Nuba soul: rock honey, like that promised by God to his people in Psalm 81. Why rock honey?, I used to ask myself, until the Nuba offered me genuine rock honey as a sign of the most exquisite hospitality they could possibly offer to a visitor on their mountains. It is precious, rare and hard to get from the most impervious rock crevices. Rock honey is the most appropriate image of the sentiments of this people. Happy is the one who receives the honey of their friendship. I myself have never felt more secure than when spending a night in a Nuba shelter.

Traditional wrestling took many elements from traditional religion, like smearing the bodies with ash, or hitting the ground with tree branches to keep evil spirits at bay, as well as the religious atmosphere permeating the actual wrestling match. Religiosity attains its strongest moments in the relation with the dead, which the Nuba share with the rest of traditional Africa. Together with Jibril or Chalu I saw myself places where libations of merissa had taken place as an offering to the dead. The graves were not marked visibly, but identifying signs stood out here and there. Passing by a rounded rock, Jibril pointed out: "This is the cemetery." Beer had been poured on the stone, with pieces of chicken and flour. The libation was still fresh. On the hilltop that dominates the school at Kerker there is a flat altar-like stone on a heap of rocks. The horizontal slab still showed traces of animal blood, despite their assuring me that the place was no longer used for traditional sacrifices. A goat skull hung from the tree that gave shade to the place. And a few paces beyond, Christians had planted a cross.

For Yousif Kuwa, cultural identity was an essential dimension of the struggle for the dignity and the rights of his people. But he did not take it as a pretext for confrontation, but as a stimulus for creativity and even for forgiveness, which is consistent with the thought of Nyerere. Julie Flint was close to him during the last weeks of his life. She reports:

> Yousif Kuwa belonged to a type of person very rare in every society, but particularly in a poor and struggling one: he was a loved leader. It was an extraordinary experience for me to go back with him to the Nuba Mountains after his first trip to Europe in 1995, and see the genuine joy with which he was received. He was not just a leader. He was everybody's friend.
>
> His vocation was that of a teacher. His dream was to retire to cultivate his garden after the end of hostilities. He struggled for the whole of his life for a just peace, not only for the Nuba but also for all the Sudanese, without distinction of race, sex or religion. He told me of when he was a student in Khartoum. While in a friend's house, he overheard the friend's daughter telling her brother: "You are a very good singer, pity that you are black." Such an event convinced him to reject the government's policy of assimilation. He said, "We shall build our civilisation, after which I will forgive all those who have humiliated us."
>
> Yousif was a great witness of the pride and trust that the Nuba entertain towards their Africanness. He showed that armed struggle is compatible with the respect for human rights and with a civil society. He was convinced that in the circumstances of the moment armed struggle was the only way for the Nuba to survive while remaining themselves, but respected all those who left the mountains to join the government garrisons. For there they had access to food, clothing and medicines.
>
> Yousif wanted self-determination for his people. The Nuba ought to have been able to choose the type of government that fitted them best, and those who would head such government. For him liberation meant the respect for everyone's rights. In 1995, during the May celebrations for the anniversary of the SPLA insurgency, I heard him exclaim: "You must struggle for your rights! And if Yousif Kuwa were to deny them to you, struggle to get them back!"

Ramadan Orandi, close collaborator of Kuwa, runs a centre of Tira culture. "We have realised," he says, "that people spoke Arabic more and more often, and that we risked losing our Tira language and culture. We began to meet, and drafted guidelines to keep our culture. Some of us are codifying the alphabet, and gathering material to publish textbooks for the various classes."

Stephen Amin, who has also gone through his own cultural itinerary, is pleasantly surprised at this renaissance:

> The government did not expect the Nuba to rebel. They thought they had killed Nuba culture: very few dared to admit their Nuba culture outside those mountains. But Yousif Kuwa and others organised the revolt, and gave back an identity and a new strength to our culture.

Martha Ousman, whom I found guarding a mountain pass with his automatic weapon, spread his arm over the expanse of the valley down below and said: "I am a Nuba, this is where I was born and nobody will ever come here to tell me what to do in my land."

One of his fellow soldiers had said more or less the same thing. He was William "Shaker" Kuali, in reality much more adept at playing the guitar than at squeezing the trigger of the Kalashnikov. It was August 1995, during my first visit to the Nuba Mountains. Everybody felt impelled to smile and dance every time he picked the strings of his guitar. And everybody was his fan on his entering the wrestling arena. Shaker told me of his passion for singing and poetry, and of his determination to turn the Sudan into a place where people of different cultures and religions could live in harmony. "My place is here, in the struggle for a better tomorrow," he said. When I returned I learned that Shaker would no longer sing his songs of hope and freedom. A few days after our meeting, on August 18, he had fallen in battle while defending his village.

My African-ness

My brothers,
With thousand of my apologies
Forgive me,
Forgive me for my frankness
For my courage.

Let me tell you
Despite all the talk,
About my Arabism
My religion,
My culture.....
I am a Nuba,
I am black,
I am African.

African-ness is my identity
It is entrenched
In my appearance
Engraved in lips
And manifested by my skin.

My African-ness
Is in the sound
Of my footstep
It is in my bewildered past
And in the depth of my laughter.

Brothers,
Forgive me
For my frankness and courage,
Despite my grandfather's humiliation,
Despite my grandmother's sale into slavery
Despite my ignorance
My backwardness
My naivety...
My tomorrow shall come.

I shall crown
My identity with knowledge
I shall light my candle.
In its light
I shall build my civilisation,
And at that time
I shall extend my hand,
I shall forgive those who tried
To destroy my identity,
Because my aspirations
Are love and peace!

Yousif Kuwa Mekki

Chronology

Important dates in the modern history of Sudan

1820 Introduction of Turko-Egyptian administration.

1839 South Sudan conquered by the Turko-Egyptian power. Commerce was introduced mainly in the form of salve trade (only formally abolished in Egypt and Sudan in 1860).

1857. Catholic Missionaries from the Don Mazza Institute arrive. One of the five priests is Daniel Comboni, father of modern Catholicism in Sudan.

1885 January – Conquest of Khartoum and the overthrow of the Turko-Egyptian administration by the Mahdi. The Mahdist state is founded. The Mahdi's forces have sufficient arms to keep the South, but not enough to subdue it, which causes an ongoing war.

1898 Battle of Omdurman. Lord Kitchener defeats Khalifa Abdalla Al-taishi (the Mahdi's successor) and his dervishes, and begins to re-conquer Sudan.

1899 – 19ᵗʰ January – Anglo-Egyptian protectorate begins the abolition of slavery.

1903 The British administration gives every missionary group that applies to work in Sudan a separate territory to evangelise. The North stays under Islamic influence.

1930 The British introduces a separatist political policy (Closed Districts Ordinance) for South Sudan, Southern Blue Nile and Nuba Mountains. The South is separated from the North avoiding the Arabisation of the South.

1936 Anglo-Egyptian treaty that confirms the Protectorate Agreement of 1899.

1943 Rival nationalists groups organise themselves into political parties: the foundation of the Umma party and Ashiqqa party (supporting the Egyptians).

1946 Annulment of the Southern policy resulting from pressure from the North.

1947 Juba Conference sees the agreement between North and South on the basis of national unity and the South participation in the legislative Assembly.

1951 King Farouk proclaims himself King of Egypt and Sudan.

1952 Self-government Statute.

1953 End of the protectorate. Anglo-Egyptian agreement on the right to self-determination and the improvement in the self-government phase. The South, not having its own political party, has no say in the matter.

5-25 November – Parliamentary elections.

1954 – 6 January – Al-Azhari elected Prime Minister.

October – Commission nominations for Sudanisation: the South get only 6 out of 800 administration positions.

1955 The conflicts begin. In August there is a mutiny in Torit, the Anya-nya secessionist movement is born. In December the resolution declaring Sudan's independence is approved.

1956 The Parliamentary regime commences. Sudan becomes a member of the Arab League. Abdallah Khalil is elected Prime Minister.

12 November – Sudan becomes a member of the UN.

1957 A Constitution is proposed providing for Islam as the State religion and Arabic as the national language.

1958 All South-Sudanese members leave Parliament when Constituent Assembly refuses the Federation proposal. War and military dictatorship increases.

1959 Sudan signs an agreement with Egypt for the Nile's water.

1964 – Foreign missionaries are expelled from South Sudan.

October 21 – The "October Revolution" leads to transitional government that oversees elections and the return of democracy.

1969 – May The "May Revolution": Gaafar Mohamed Nimeiry mounts a coup in collaboration with the communist party.

1971 – July 19 Nimeiry becomes President.

1972 – March 27 Nimeiry for the government and Joseph Lagu for the rebels sign the Addis Ababa peace agreement. The Regional Self-

Government Act by the southern provinces becomes part of the Sudanese Constitution in 1973. Civil war ends after 17 years. An Executive Council for the South is appointed.

October – Southern Regional Assembly elections; in the South the first legally elected government is established, with Abel Alier as the first President.

1978 – April 12 – The National Reconciliation Agreement is signed between political opposition (National Front of Hassan Al-Turabi) and government.

1979 Riots and strikes in Khartoum and other cities asking for higher incomes and lower life-costs. Students ask for free press. Hassan al-Turabi appointed as Attorney General.

1983 – 16 May Mutiny at Bor, under the leadership of Kerubino Kwanyin Bol. It is the official birth date of the Sudan People Liberation Movement/Army (SPLM/A). Shortly after John Garang takes over the leadership. Civil war restarts: South-Sudanese rise up against Nimeiry's proclamation of the Shari'ah (Islamic law).

1986-1989 Sadiq al-Mahdi is prime Minster.

1989 – June 30 – Military coup by General Omar al-Bashir, who becomes the new President.

1991 May In Ethiopia the fall of Haile Mariam Mengistu "the red negus", deprives SPLA of important political and logistical support.

August Riek Machar, Lam Akol and Gordon Kong proclaim the deposition of Garang. The SPLM/A is split in two factions.

1992 January A *fatwa* (Islamic sentence) is issued by Northern Muslims against the Nuba, and a jihad (holy war) is proclaimed against them.

1995 Northern opposition groups join the Southern fighters.

1998 Heavy famine and water shortage in the South bring a great number of deaths.

1999 – February Yousif Kuwa visits Italy, where he has meetings in the Italian Minsitry of Foreign Affairs, in the Vatican and with the Foreign Affairs Committee of the Italian Parliament.

September Sudan begins to export oil. In December President Bashir dissolves the National Assembly and declares a state of emergency following a power struggle with parliamentary speaker, his Islamic opponent, Hassan al-Turabi.

2000 December – New elections (boycotted by opposition) re-elect Bashir for President of the Republic for another five years. State of emergency is renewed. Fighting between government and rebels continues. Bombings in the South increase.

2001 February – Islamic leader Hassan al-Turabi arrested a day after his party, the Popular National Congress, signed a memorandum of understanding with the southern rebel Sudan People's Liberation Army (SPLA).

2001-March 31 – Yousif Kuwa dies in a London Hospital.

2001-April - May – SPLA rebels threaten to attack international oil workers brought in by the government to help exploit vast new oil reserves. Governmental troops are accused of trying to drive civilians and rebels from the oilfields. In April and May there are more arrests of PNC members. The Government forces launch a heavy military offence aiming to crash the rebellion in the Nuba Mountains. They almost reach Yousif Kuwa tomb. Under the leadership of Kuwa successor, Abdelaziz Adam el-Hilu, the attack is repulsed.

2001 June – Failure of Nairobi peace talks attended by President al-Bashir and John Garang.

2001 July – Government says it accepts a Libyan/Egyptian initiative to end the civil war. The plan includes a national reconciliation conference and reforms. Bamboo oil field inaugurated in Unity State, producing 15,000 barrels per day.

2001 September – UN lifts sanctions against Sudan, imposed in 1996 over accusations that Sudan harboured suspects who attempted to kill Egyptian President Hosni Mubarak.

2002 –19 January At Bürgenstock, in Switzerland, representatives of the Khartoum Government and SPLM/A leadership from the Nuba Mountians sign a ceasefire. A Joint Military Commission (JMC), with international monitors, is put in charge to supervise the implementation of the ceasefire.

2002 July 20 After talks in Kenya, government and SPLA sign the Machakos Protocol, a preliminary understanding on ending the 19-year civil war. Government accepts the right of self-determination for South Sudan after six-year interim period. Southern rebels accept application of Shari'ah law in the north.

2002 July 27 President al-Bashir and SPLA leader John Garang meet face-to-face for the first time, through the mediation of Ugandan President Yoweri Museveni.

2002 October – Government and SPLA agree on a ceasefire for the duration of negotiations. Despite this, hostilities continue in the South, while in the Nuba Mountains the ceasefire holds.

2003 October – PNC leader Turabi released after nearly three years in detention and the ban on his party is lifted.

2004 January – Army moves to quell rebel uprising in western region of Darfur; more than 100,000 people escape to Chad. In the meantime, peace talks continue in Kenya

2004 March – Official sources at the UN affirm that 'government' militias "Janjawid" were carrying out systematic assassination of African civilians throughout Darfur. Army officials and opposition politicians amongst which Turabi, are arrested on the accusation of planning a coup.

2004 May – The conflicts in Darfur spill over into Chad, where the local armed forces clash with the Arab militias on the side of the Khartoum government. At Naivasha the Sudanese government and the SPLA sign the protocols to end of the civil war. The agreements also confront the questions of power allocation in the New Sudan and sharing of resources (oil and others) between the North and South.

2004 September – The UN envoy announces that Sudan hasn't kept its promise to disarm the Arab militias in Darfur and that it must accept help from the international community to protect the civilians in the region. US Secretary of State Colin Powell declares that the tragedy in Darfur could be considered as genocide.

2004 October – Peace talks resume in Kenya between the government and the SPLM, after an interruption of two months. Kofi Annan organizes the creation of an Enquiry Commission to investigate and discover whether genocide has been perpetrated in Darfur. The job of leading the commission is conferred on Antonio Cassese, the first President of the International Criminal Court for former Yugoslavia. The African Union decides to increase its presence in Darfur and to send a civilian police force.

2004 November 7 – The Sudanese government accepts putting an end to the military flights over Darfur and signs a series of agreements in the Nigerian city of Abuja, regarding military and humanitarian issues. On November 19, the government and the SPLM sign an agreement protocol in which they promise before the UN to conclude a comprehensive peace agreement before the end of the year.

2005, January 9 – SPLM/A and the Khartoum government sign in the Kenyan capital, Nairobi, a Comprehensive Peace Agreement that puts an end to war between them. But the conflict continues in Darfur.

Bibliography

African Rights, *A Desolate Peace: Human Rights in the Nuba Mountains,* African Rights, London 1997.

African Rights, *Facing Genocide: The Nuba of Sudan,* African Rights, London 1995.

AKOL, LAM, SPLM/A, *Inside an African Revolution,* Khartoum University Press, Khartoum 2001

ARKELL, ANTHONY J., *A History of the Sudan to A.D. 1821,* University of London, London 1955.

BAUMANN, GERD, *National Integration and Local Integrity: the Miri of the Nuba Mountains in the Sudan,* Clarendon Press, Oxford 1987.

BOK, FRANCIS, *Escape from Slavery: The True Story of My Ten Years in Captivity – And My Journey to Freedom in America,* St. Martin's Press, New York 2003 (with Edward Tivnan).

BURCKHARDT, JOHANN LUDWIG, *Travels in Nubia,* African Association, London 1819.

BYARUHANGA-AKIIKI, ANATOLI B.T., et al, *Cast Away Fear: A Contribution to the African Synod,* New People Media Centre, Nairobi 1994.

CARROLL, SCOTT T., "Wrestling in Ancient Nubia", in *Journal of Sport History,* vol. 15, n. 2, North American Society for Sport History, 1988, pp. 121-137.

DENG, FRANCIS MADING, *War of Visions. Conflict of Identities in the Sudan,* The Brookings Institute, Washington 1995.

FARIS, JAMES C., *Nuba Personal Art*, University of Toronto Press, Toronto 1972.

FARIS, JAMES C., *Southeast Nuba Social Relations*, Edition Herodot Alano Verlag, Aachen 1989.

IAN MACKIE, *Trek into Nuba*, Pentland Press, Edinburgh 1994.

IBRAHIM, AHMED UTHMAN MUHAMMAD, *The Dilemma of British Rule in the Nuba Mountains: 1898-1947*, University of Khartoum, Khartoum 1985.

ITEN, OSWALD, *Fungor: Ein Nuba-Dorf wird ruiniert*, Ullstein, Berlin 1983.

JAKOBI, ANGELIKA' KUMMERLE, TANJA, *The Nubian Languages. An Annotated Bibliography*, Rudiger Kope Verlag, Colonia 1993.

JOHNSON, DOUGLAS H., *The Root Causes of Sudan's Civil Wars*, James Currey, Oxford 2003.

KOINONIA NUBA, *Once Upon a Time in the Nuba Mountains*, Koinonia Nuba, Nairobi 2004.

KRIZNAR, TOMO, *Nuba: cisti ljudie*, Samozalozba, Lubiana 1999.

NADEL, SIEGFRIED F., *The Nuba*, Oxford University Press, London-New York/Toronto 1947.

NYABA, PETER A., *The Politics of Liberation in South Sudan: An Insider's View*, Fountain Publishers, Kampala 1997.

PALLME, IGNATIUS, *Travels in Kordofan*, J. Madden and Co., London 1844.

RAHHAL, SULEIMAN MUSA, *The Right to Be Nuba: The Story of Sudanese People's Struggle for Survival*, Red Sea Press, Asmara/ Lawrenceville (New Jersey), 2001.

RODGER, GEORGE, *Village of the Nubas*, Phaidon, London 1949.

SCROGGINS, DEBORAH, *Emma's War: An Aid Worker, Radical Islam and the Politics of Oil – A True Story of Love and Death in the Sudan*, Pantheon, New York 2002.

SELIGMAN, CHARLES G., "The Physical Characters of the Nuba of Kordofan", in *Journal of the Royal Anthropological Institute of Great Britain and Ireland*, 40, London 1910.

STEVENSON, RONALD C., *The Nuba People of Kordofan Province,* University of Khartoum, Khartoum 1984.

WHEELER, ANDREW C. *Announcing the Light: Sudanese Witnesses to the Gospel,* Paulines Publications Africa, Nairobi 1998.

Documentaries

ANNECHINI, PAOLO and BAROLO, LUCA, *Kizito, I Monti Nuba, il Sudan,* 18', Telepace, Verona 1998.

BIONDETTI, ALBERTO and SPILLARI, ALESSIO, *Nuba. Popolo di uomini,* 60', Verona 2001.

Campagna italiana per la pace il rispetto dei diritti umani in Sudan, *Sudan: acqua, petrolio e una guerra... che non e di religione,* 17', Luci nel mondo, Verona 2001.

D'AYBAURY, HUGO, *The Right to be Nuba,* 45', Peekaboo Pictures, London 1994.

DEMICHELIS, DAVIDE, *I Nuba del Sudan,* 52', Comunita Nuova, Milano 1996.

FLINT, JULIE, *The Nuba. Sudan's Secret War,* 45', BBC, London 1995.

FLINT, JULIE, *Commander Yousif Kuwa Mekke,* 65', London 2002.

HOWES, ARTHUR and HARDIE, AMY, *Kafi's Story,* 56', London 1989.

HOWES, ARTHUR, *Nuba Conversations,* 52', London 2000.

HOWES, ARTHUR, *Benjamin and his Brother,* 87', London 2002.

KRIZNAR, TOMO and WEISS, MAJA, *Nuba, Pure People,* Bela Film, Lubiana 1999.

KRIZNAR, TOMO, *Nuba. Voices from the other side,* 55', Radiotelevizija Slovenija, Lubiana 2001.

LEWIS, DAMIEN, *The Oil Wars,* 18', Wow Ltd., London 1999.

LEWIS, DAMIEN, *Death in the Air,* 7', Wow Ltd., London 2000.

MONTRANARO, SILVESTRO, *E poi ho incontrato Madid,* 57', Rai, Roma 1999.

NARCISO, CARLOS, *Dignidade, 32'*, SIC, Lisbon 1999

PICCOLI, CAMILLO E SOAVE, PATRICK, *Un genocidio invisibile,* 27', Telepace, Verona 1999

Internet Resources

Amani: www.amaniforafrica.org

Appeal to the United Nations for the Nuba people
www.peacelink.it/africa/appnubai.html

BELL, HERMAN, *The Nuba Mountains: Who Spoke What in 1976?*
www.hf.uib.no/smi/sa/tan/nuba.html

BURR, MILLARD, *Quantifying Genocide in Southern Sudan and the Nuba Mountains,* 1983-1998
www.refugees.org/news/crisis/sudan.pdf

Campagna italiana per la pace e il rispetto dei diritti umani in Sudan
www.campagnasudan.it

Human Rights Watch/Africa, *Civilian Devastation: Abuses by All Parties in the War in Southern Sudan,* July 1993
www.hrw.org/reports/193/sudan
See also www.hrw.org/doc/?t=africa&c=sudan)
Koinonia italy.peacelink.org/mappa/group_7.html

Les églises au Soudan: www.eglisesoudan.org

Nuba Survival: www.nubasurvival.org

Oil & Human Rights in Central and Southern Sudan. A geographic *resource*
www.rightsmaps.com/html/sudmap1.html

Peacelink: www.peacelink.it

The Nuba Mountains Homepage: leden.tref.nl/~ende0098

THELWALL, ROBIN and SCHADEBERG, THILO C., *The Linguistic Settlement of the Nuba Mountains*
www.thenubian.net/settlement.php

Vigilance Soudan: www.vigilsd.org